GET A REEL JOB

Finding Your First
Writing • Producing • Directing • Acting • Crew Position
in The Film Industry

By

Philip Nemy

Published By Angel's Touch Productions
22906 Calabash Street
Woodland Hills, CA 91364

Copyright © 1999 by Philip Nemy
Cover Design Copyright © by David McPherson
First Printing 1999
Printed in the United States of America
ISBN 0-9669443-6-4

FOR MOM & DAD

WARNING - DISCLAIMER

I wrote this book with the intention of providing information on how to find one's first job in the film industry in Los Angeles. I sell it to you with the understanding that I am not rendering to you any legal, accounting or any other professional services. Should you need any legal or expert services, then you should seek the services of competent professionals and/or experts.

You are urged to read the entire book, regardless of whether it directly relates to your interests or not, learn as much as possible about the film industry, and tailor the information you have accumulated to your own specific needs.

I have worked very hard to make this book as complete and accurate as I can. No matter how hard I try, there may still be a few mistakes in spelling, punctuation, grammar, formatting, and possibly even in content. With that in mind, when reading this book, recognize that it should be used as a guide and not the definitive word on the film industry, up to the date of printing.

The reason I wrote this book is two-fold: to educate and entertain. Both myself and the publisher shall have neither liability nor the responsibility to any person or entity with respect to loss or damage caused, or alleged to be caused, directly or indirectly by the information contained in this book.

If you do not wish to be bound by the above, you may return this book to the publisher for a full refund.

TABLE OF CONTENTS

Order Form

INDEX OF FIGURES

ACKNOWLEDGMENTS

Thanks must be given to a number of individuals without whose support and assistance this book would not have been completed. First of all, thank you Mark Helm for planting the thought in my head many moons ago that I could, in fact, write a book.

I am grateful for the assistance of my father, Alfred Nemy, for reading and critiquing the many drafts of this work. His many hours of careful study pouring over the manuscript looking for spelling errors, questioning the clarity of sections, and reminding me to "talk to the reader as if he knows nothing about your industry," have been immeasurable.

This book benefitted greatly from the careful editorial guidance of Joe Gomez, Sarah Fain and Kathy Zotnowski. Joe took the time out of his busy teaching schedule to carefully review this book, page after page, looking for errors, omissions, clarity issues, and offering solid criticism. I am truly indebted. Sarah gave valuable input from a film student point of view, offering solid advice and suggestions. Kathy painstakingly went through the book page by page correcting my many grammatical and spelling errors. All three of these individuals recognized early on the value of such a book as this and provided unfailing support and encouragement.

I must also extend thanks to Michael Rostker for his patient tutoring of me on Pagemaker Software, without which I could not have actually laid out this book, and thanks to Susan Bradley who offered valuable advice, suggestions and guidance on the world of publishing and marketing of books. Her style, enthusiasm and knowledge is amazing.

Many thanks to the many film industry professionals from whom I received valuable input and helpful suggestions, including Chip Diggins, Deborah Barylski, Adam Marcus, Virginia Hoyt, Mark Indig, Stephanie Mangano, and Tony Aveta.

I must also thank Marty Katz, Mark Bakshi, Karen MacKain, Sam Mercer, Richard Rothschild, Su Armstrong, Peter Bogart, Paul Steinke, Scott Nicolaides, Whitney Green and Bruce Hendricks for their teachings and their support. I offer this book as a testament to your expertise and gift for teaching.

And finally, a big thank you to God, who provides me daily with constructive criticism to help me grow, and whose love and support has encouraged me to keep plugging ahead to see this book published.

Philip Nemy
1999

FOREWORD

I wish a book like this had been written 15 years ago when I was beginning my career. Had it been available, I would have saved myself time, money, frustration and many headaches.

Not very long ago, I was in the same position as you are now. I believed I had talent, I had worked in the New York theater world as a beginning actor, stage manager and director, but I had an overwhelming desire to try Hollywood. And yet two questions still concerned me: "Was it time to go west?", and "Knowing no one in Los Angeles, if I made the move, how would I find work?"

I made the decision to go to Los Angeles almost arbitrarily. A friend who had gone to film school called me to say he was moving to Hollywood and did I want to join him? I wasn't making much of a living in the theater, and I was frustrated by my inability to progress further in my career. So I headed west with my friend, with the courage to face the unknown knowing I would confront it with a companion.

You probably face a similar situation or will seriously consider it in the near future: do I move to Los Angeles or not? *I know what you're thinking, I've been there.* And I can tell you this: although film production outside of California has dramatically increased over the last few years with new film production appearing in Pennsylvania, Illinois, North Carolina, Southern Florida, Texas, and even internationally in Vancouver, British Columbia and Toronto, Ontario, the bottom line is that the decisions to finance and produce a film are still made in Los Angeles. If you want a career in the film industry, eventually you'll have to go Los Angeles.

This holds true for all the players in the industry. If you're an actor, you may ultimately act in front of the camera at a location in Dallas, Texas, but you'll most certainly have to audition in LA. If you're a writer, you can have the luxury of writing your screenplay anywhere in the world. But in order to get it produced, the people you must sell to all work out of LA. And the same can be said of almost any profession in the film industry: directing, producing, editing, costume design, production design, etc.

I've written this book with the intent of keeping you from making the same false starts that I made when I started my career. For example, it cost more than I expected and took longer than planned to travel from New York to Los Angeles. And while it was nice to have all my belongings and furniture with me, I could have saved time, money, and energy if I had brought only what I truly needed.

I sent out hundreds of letters and resumes to anyone working in the industry whose address I could obtain, only to discover that my resume was incorrectly prepared, my cover letter was too vague and unfocused, and the majority of the people I mailed to were the wrong people to contact in the first place. Over time, I discovered that my "shotgun" approach was less effective than an intelligently planned "rifle shot."

By taking a class in networking (the art of using contacts to help you get you what you want), I quickly learned how important it is to meet people and maintain relationships, no matter how big or small, no matter how indirectly related to your final goal they are. These experiences of trial and error could have been dramatically decreased, and my employment opportunities could have greatly increased, had I had a book such as this to help me.

Whether you are planning to move to Los Angeles in the near future, or just beginning to seriously consider a career in film, but not quite ready to make the move, this book will help you prepare for the inevitable by addressing three key areas: moving to and living in Los Angeles, equipping yourself with the basic tools for finding employment, and how to compete in Hollywood.

For purposes of making the book easy to read, I have chosen to write using masculine terms such as he, him or his, rather than he/she, him/her or his/hers. The suggestions and advice I offer in this book are valid for all individuals regardless of sex. No oversight is intended or implied.

One last thing. For this book to be helpful to others in the future, it must grow, be revised, and updated with the valuable new information only your experiences can provide. If you learn something along the way that you feel is important enough to let others know about, and you'd like to have it published in future, updated copies of this book, please feel free to write down your thoughts and send them to me in care of the address below. Your future colleagues will appreciate that you took the time to share with them some advice, a few suggestions, and even a couple of hints about how to "Get A Reel Job".

Philip Nemy
c/o Angel's Touch Productions
22906 Calabash Street
Woodland Hills, CA 91364
E-mail: captainnemo2@earthlink.net

INTRODUCTION

As a recent graduate from college, or simply an ardent fan of film, you have undoubtedly invested some time focusing on the craft, the techniques, and the art form of the film industry. However, should you choose to enter this industry, get ready - you're about to enter a completely different world where the focus is on "the product and the box office." This different world is the "business" end of the world of entertainment. After all, they call it "Show Business" not "Show Art." In this world you have to deal with the nitty-gritty questions and problems of everyday living, seeking some sort of employment income, while selling yourself to the industry.

The beginning of this book is structured to take you through each step in finding your first job in the film industry. It assumes that you have made the decision to move to Los Angeles, or are seriously considering a move out West. Regardless of what level of readiness you are in, there are many key factors to consider: getting to Los Angeles; finding an apartment; preparing resumes; getting an agent; etc. Each is a necessary step in becoming a successful player in this industry, regardless of what position you aim to hold.

After taking care of all of this, you can then move on to the main goal, the reason you came to Los Angeles, getting the "reel" job as an actor, a writer, a director, etc. Since not everyone will be seeking the same career, the subsequent parts of the book are split into sections dealing with the different careers: writers, producers, directors, crew and studio personnel, and actors. As part of your ongoing education about filmmaking, I've chosen to present these sections in the same sequence as they occur in making a film.

First, nothing happens until there is a screenplay. A writer must have an idea which he develops into a story, and ultimately stretches the story into a screenplay. He then begins the search for a producer who can help him raise the financing for the screenplay to be produced.

Producers can be found in many forms: individuals who excel in the art of salesmanship and who can sell the screenplay to a studio; a producer can raise funds independently from a variety of companies and individuals who wish to invest in films; even the studios themselves can act as producers by developing their own ideas and hiring writers to execute them.

Once the producer and writer have agreed to work together to get the screenplay produced, and the necessary funds have been raised, either independently or through a studio, a director is hired. It is the director's vision that we ultimately see on screen. He must assemble a team of collaborators (editor, director of photography, production designer, costume designer, etc.) to assist him with translating the screenplay into visual images. Once the collaborators have been chosen, their support crew can be selected. This includes everyone from the Production Manager to the electricians to the Production Assistants.

And finally, having held extensive auditions to find the right cast, the actors are hired, photography begins, and the actors act. Although greatly simplified, this is the normal process a film undergoes from idea to screenplay to production. Naturally, then, the first section after THE BASICS starts with THE WRITER.

LOS ANGELES:
THE FILM CAPITAL OF THE WORLD

MOVING EXPENSES

If you're considering moving to Los Angeles, don't just buy a plane ticket or jump in a car as I did and head out west. There's a lot to think about and do before you actually leave town.

Obtaining an Automobile

First, you must have a car. LA is so spread out, and the public transportation system is so limited, you will need a car to get around town. If you don't own a car, then you need to save up for one *before* you come to Los Angeles.

You'll save money initially if you purchase and register your car anywhere but in California. California has expensive automobile registration ($150-250 annually) and requires a smog check fee every other year ($25-50). The state also requires proof of auto insurance, which can cost as much as $2000 or more annually, depending upon your driving record.

If you do plan to drive to Los Angeles, I cannot emphasize enough that you should make sure your car is in good working condition. Driving out to Los Angeles from the East Coast is a *long, long* drive, generally 3-5 days, depending upon your starting point. There's nothing worse than having your car break down on a high-speed Interstate Highway late at night somewhere in the middle of the U.S. with no one around to help you repair it.

With that in mind, you may wish to purchase a membership in an automobile club. One of the largest clubs, and the one with the most local offices nationwide is AAA, the Automobile Association of America. Membership varies from state to state, but the services in one office are generally the same in every office in the US. A membership in AAA in California runs roughly $35 per year with membership being honored at all AAA offices in the US and Canada. The membership fee may be higher or lower in your neighborhood. AAA provides a wide variety of services, such as 24 hour emergency road service, at little or no charge to their members.

In addition, they will prepare a "Trip-Tik" based on information you furnish them about where you're headed. The Trip-Tik includes a map of the best route to travel, where road construction and most speed traps are located, the most inexpensive AAA-approved hotels along the route (most AAA-approved hotels offer discounts to AAA members), and choice restaurants along the way. They will even provide you with American Express Travelers Cheques at no charge. AAA also provides its members with other services including free city, state, regional, and national maps, DMV registration, traffic citation processing, new and used automobile pricing and information.

However, the most important service you may need while traveling across country is the AAA's toll-free 800 number which you can call for dependable road service anywhere in the US or Canada in case your automobile breaks down. For those occasions when you break down far from an available pay phone, AAA will rent you a cellular telephone. For a very nominal fee, these cellular phones can be used anywhere in the US where cellular service is available. This excellent safety measure may just get you out of a tough spot on the road. Check your local AAA office for more information about this feature.

AAA is not the only automotive club out there. Allstate, Amoco, Exxon, Chevron and many others all have Travel Clubs whose membership services and pricing are competitive to that of AAA. Take a good look at the other competitors before making up your mind about which service to use.

What to Take With You

Once you have a car, you can begin planning what you need to take with you. Take only your clothes and the minimal items that fit in your trunk or a small trailer towed behind your car. Don't take everything you own as I did - you won't need it! Plus, it's expensive to bring all that stuff with you! Chances are you won't find a place to live in LA quickly, so it'll cost you to store your possessions in a safe place. Parking a trailer on the street is an invitation to theft. Since you won't be bringing a bed, remember to bring a sleeping bag and pillow so you'll have something to sleep in or on when you get into an apartment for the first time.

If it turns out that your belongings (and those of a traveling companion, if you wisely don't try this trip alone) won't all fit in a car, the most reasonable approach is to rent a small trailer to tow behind your automobile. Based on 1999 rates, U-Haul will rent you a 6' x 12' trailer one-way for approximately $850. You must place a $20 refundable deposit at least 24 hours in advance with a credit card, or 72 hours in advance when using cash as your deposit. Rental prices vary from company to company, so shop around before you settle on a rental trailer.

Towing a trailer will put some drag on your automobile and cause it to use gas more quickly, but the cost of gasoline is a lot cheaper than renting a truck. But be careful. Don't put a greater load on your car's engine than it's capable of pulling. A four cylinder Geo wasn't designed to pull a heavily loaded trailer! It's important to check your car's owner's manual to insure that your car is capable of pulling a trailer.

However, if you must rent a truck, then shop around for one. Based on 1999 rates, Ryder Truck Rental will rent you a 15' moving van one-way for approximately $1,500, which includes 10 travel days and 3,400 miles. Each mile after that is $0.60/mile. You must place an $80 refundable deposit at least 24 hours in advance with a credit card, or 72 hours in advance when using cash as your deposit. Furniture pads rent at $15 for a dozen and a hand-truck or dolly will also cost $15. If a 15' truck is too big for you, a 10' moving van rents for about $1,400.

On the Road

Once your truck or car is loaded, you're off! *I would very strongly suggest not traveling alone.* Travel with someone you know. There is safety in numbers, and you can share the driving load on the long trip. You can also split the moving costs with one or more fellow travelers.

If you are the type that has a "lead foot" and tends to drive over the legal speed limit, then you might want to look into purchasing a radar detector (starting at approx. $65). Some of the Interstate Highways out West have very long stretches where it is easy to lose sight of the speed limit. Make sure you check with AAA to find out in which states the use of a radar detector is illegal. I'm glad I did that, since driving long distances on interstates tends to be hynotic and you do tend to speed.

It's a long trip, so don't try to do it non-stop. It will take approximately 3-5 days to travel from the East Coast to Los Angeles. Enjoy the drive, watch the scenery, visit some tourist sites along the way - you may not get a chance to see the country this way for a very long time. If you really need to watch your check book, you may be tempted to sleep in your car or truck by pulling into a road-side truck stop, but you need to know that this can be very dangerous, and I *do not recommend it*, particularly if you're driving alone. A safer consideration may be to stay at a Travel Lodge, Motel 6, or similar economy motels for about $30/night. Travel Lodge has a 24 hour reservation line: 1-800-255-3050.

FINDING HOUSING IN LOS ANGELES

When you arrive in Los Angeles, you'll be exhausted from the long drive. I sure was. You'll need to rest and sleep. When I moved out, I stayed with a friend of my traveling partner. But if you don't have a friend or relative in town, where do you go? Try the Glendale YMCA (818-240-4130) which rents rooms to both men and women at about $20.90/night. Or try a low cost motel in Hollywood or the San Fernando Valley. It doesn't have to be gorgeous, just a place to spend the night.

Because the city is so spread out, you need to be smart about looking for housing. Otherwise, the search could take forever and cost a ton of money. First, ask yourself these questions:

• what kind of housing do I want? - apartment, duplex or triplex, condo, townhouse, detached home, or guest house (a guest house is a small studio or one-bedroom residence usually located behind the main house on the same property. Often it is a garage that has been converted into a living space).

• how much rent can I afford per month?

• how big a place do I want? - a studio, 1 bedroom, 2 bedroom etc.

• in which area of Los Angeles do I want to live?

If you're uncertain of the area of Los Angeles in which you want to live, friends or relatives who already live in Los Angeles might be able to offer recommendations. I'll go into this topic later in this section. Once you've answered these questions, you can begin your search.

Resource Guides

The two best sources for available housing are The Recycler weekly newspaper, which costs $1.75 and comes out on Thursday mornings, and the Classified section of the *Los Angeles Times* newspaper which costs $0.25 weekdays and $1 on Sundays. Stay away from rental services which provide you with listings of rental properties throughout the city for an up-front fee. Experience tells me they're a rip-off.

Metropolitan Los Angeles is one of the largest land-masses in North America. The distance from the farthest side of Los Angeles County in the northwest to the farthest side of Orange County in the southeast is 100 miles, with the area equaling 8,000 square miles. However, if you intend to work in the film industry, you probably will want to stay in Los Angeles County to limit your traveling.

To better understand the layout of Metropolitan Los Angeles, it would be wise to purchase a Thomas Brothers Map Guide™, published by Thomas Brothers Map Company. This Guide is a wire-bound book detailing on 8" x 10" squares the land area of Los Angeles and its streets, landmarks, highways, etc. Figure 1 illustrates part of a typical page from a Thomas Brothers Map Guide™.

The 1999 Los Angeles version of the Thomas Brothers Map Guide™ costs $18.95, while the combined Los Angeles/Orange County version will cost you $27.95. You can even purchase one with Zip Code designations for $32.95. Buy one before you arrive in LA by calling Thomas Brothers Map Company at (714) 863-1984 and having them mail a guide to you. If you choose to purchase one before you arrive, use the Appendix in the back of this book to notate people, offices, and locations

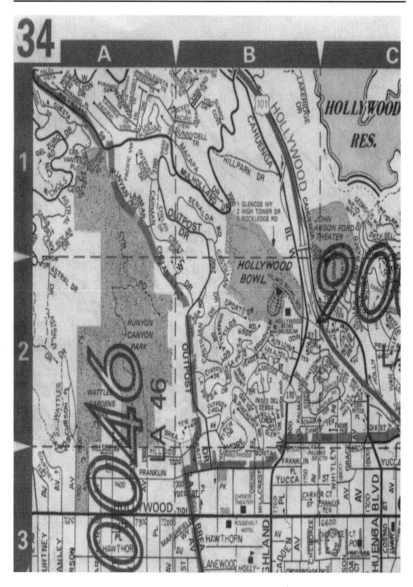

**PART OF A TYPICAL PAGE FROM A
THOMAS BROTHERS MAP GUIDE™**

FIGURE 1

that interest you. Then use your Map Guide to find these places. It will give you an idea in advance where the majority of your potential business contacts are located, and may influence where you choose to find housing.

THE COST OF HOUSING

What To Expect

In all the areas I'll be describing in this section, prices for housing vary depending upon size and location, but you can assume the following costs as general price ranges for unfurnished housing in all areas as of the fall of 1999:

- studio $450-600/month

- one bedroom $550-1300/month

- two bedroom $700-1600/month

I learned early on that housing in Los Angeles is bountiful. You will find apartments, guest houses, single-family houses, and condos available in a variety of neighborhoods and price ranges. Prices are not necessarily consistent throughout the city. For example, a one-bedroom apartment in the Van Nuys area of the San Fernando Valley may go for $550/month, while a one-bedroom apartment in another area of the San Fernando Valley called Studio City may go for $1,000/month. You can find exactly what you want provided you take the time to look.

It is common practice in Los Angeles to ask for first month's rent, last month's rent, and a security deposit that is usually equal to a month's rent. Technically, this is against the law. In Los Angeles County, a landlord can legally only ask for the first month's rent and a security deposit or the last month's rent and a security deposit, not all three. It gets tricky though, because if a landlord asks for all three and you remind him of the law, the landlord may think of you as a "troublemaker" and offer the housing to another qualified applicant. Nevertheless, it is the law.

Security deposits are refundable once you have moved out, assuming you have created no damage to the rental unit. Occasionally you are asked for a cleaning deposit of several hundred dollars and/or a key deposit which are both refundable upon moving out. You can always try to negotiate out some of these deposits, but for planning purposes, assume you will have to come up with three times the monthly rent to occupy a rental unit. For example, $500/first month's rent, $500/last month's rent, $500/security deposit, $200/cleaning fee, and a $10 key deposit, would require you to write a check for $1710 to get an apartment!! With this level of costs, you may want to consider sharing an apartment with a friend(s) or relative(s).

Signing A Lease

Once you decide on an apartment or house and *before* you sign a lease, go over the entire apartment or house with the landlord and/or superintendent and make out a list and drawing of all scratches, marks, holes, defects, etc., *anywhere* and *everywhere* in the unit. Make two copies of the list/drawing; have the landlord and/or superintendent sign both copies of the list/drawing, and write into the lease that the landlord accepts the attached list/drawing as a legally-binding part of the lease describing these specific conditions of the apartment for which you will not be held accountable to repair and/or to clean.

If you will be sharing an apartment or house with a roommate, it is important that both your names are on the lease. If only your name appears on the lease, then only you are legally liable for the lease. If your roommate skips out on you for any reason, you are still responsible for the rent. However, if two people sign the lease, then as far as the landlord is concerned, either person can be held responsible for the entire lease. This provides you with some protection: if you're roommate skips out on you, the landlord will come to you for the rent, but you'll now have a legal means by which to file suit against your ex-roommate in Small Claims Court for his share of the owed rent.

One-year leases are often requested, although you can sometimes negotiate a 6-month lease or even a month-to-month rental agreement. You can find furnished apartments, but you can also get an unfurnished apartment and wait to buy the furnishings you need and will feel comfortable with when you'll have the money.

Here are a few important things to consider when looking for an apartment:

- identify yourself by any other job than an actor! I learned the hard way that landlords are reluctant to rent to unemployed actors. Unemployed secretaries, okay, but actors - forget it!

- get an apartment that includes security parking. LA is often referred to as the car theft capital of the United States.

- find an apartment with laundry facilities. It's a pain to have to drive to a laundromat miles away.

- if you can afford it, get an apartment with air conditioning and/or ceiling fans - you'll need them in the hot summers.

- ask the landlord if he's willing to pick up some of the utilities, especially water. Water is expensive in LA and can be rationed by the city government in extreme circumstances (it happened in 1992 during a severe drought!).

- offer your services as an apartment manager or as his assistant to help cut your monthly rent.

- give yourself a few days to look for housing. Don't rush into anything you'll regret later.

- it is helpful to be employed or have a healthy bank account prior to apartment hunting. Often times, if you are unemployed, a landlord will not even consider you. But if you have a large bank account that he can go after should you default on your monthly payments, you may be okay.

AN OVERVIEW OF GREATER LOS ANGELES

Now that you have some insight into the nitty-gritty of apartment hunting, it's time to investigate some of the areas of the city in which you'll be looking. To better understand Los Angeles, we'll separate the city into regions: to the extreme northern end of Los Angeles County lies the *Santa Clarita Valley*; between the Santa Clarita Valley & the Ventura Freeway and running east & west from Glendale to Woodland Hills is the *San Fernando Valley*; south of the San Fernando Valley lie the two central areas of *Hollywood & Downtown Los Angeles*; to the west of Hollywood is the *Westside*; to the southeast of Hollywood are *The Beach Communities*; and to the east & northeast of downtown Los Angeles is the *San Gabriel Valley*.

The key thing to remember when exploring the areas of Los Angeles for housing is location: you will want to be close to the studios and areas where you'll work so that you won't spend so much time commuting and using a lot of expensive gasoline. Keep in mind that gasoline prices in Los Angeles tend to be higher than most other cities in the country, often by as much as 10-20%.

Santa Clarita Valley

Until recently, the Santa Clarita Valley was comprised of four un-incorporated regions know as Saugus, Valencia, Newhall and Canyon Country. Now it is a township known as Santa Clarita with its own mayor, city council, police department, etc. However, people still refer to the four regions by their names.

This area is home to a non-union studio facility called Valencia Studios (which was severely damaged in the January 1994 earthquake), as well as The Golden Oaks Ranch, one of the last remaining western film ranches left in California (owned by The Walt Disney Company). The Santa Clarita Valley is approximately a 1-1/2 hour drive from downtown Hollywood. Affordable housing is available in any one of the four regions, but the drive to and from Los Angeles is not fun. Remember: rush hour traffic runs from 7am to 10am and 3pm to 7pm and usually doubles your driving time. The weather in the valley is dramatic: summer often reaches 110 degrees, winter can drop to 40. The outer reaches of the valley can occasionally get snow!

San Fernando Valley

One of largest commercially developed valleys in the United States, the San Fernando Valley is home to Disney, Warner Brothers Burbank, NBC, CBS-Radford, and Universal. The Valley is bordered by the Simi Valley Freeway (US-118) and the Foothill Freeway (I-210) to the north, and the Ventura Freeway (I-101) to the south. For a better reference of this region, check your Thomas Brothers Map Guide™.

The northern portion of the Valley has a number of housing regions: Chatsworth, a community zoned for the ownership of horses; Granada Hills, single family homes and apartments; Northridge, apartments and rental houses catering to the students at Cal State University - Northridge; and Pacoima, an ethnically diverse, lower-income housing area being developed with new condos and townhouses.

The southern portion of the Valley includes these regions: Canoga Park, Reseda, Van Nuys, and North Hollywood, all with plenty of affordable housing; Burbank, home to Disney, Warner

Brothers, and NBC film and TV studios, with plenty of affordable housing; and Glendale, a quaint community tucked into the foothills of the Angeles National Forest, also with affordable housing.

The main roadway traveling from one end of the Valley to the other is Ventura Boulevard. Housing communities "south of the boulevard" and into the foothills include Calabasas, with expensive housing; Woodland Hills, a mix of expensive and moderately priced housing; Tarzana, mostly expensive single family homes; Encino, mostly expensive single family homes; Sherman Oaks, a mix of expensive and moderately priced housing with a number of guest houses available; Studio City, home to CBS-Radford Studios with a mix of expensive and moderately priced housing including a number of guest houses; and Universal City, mostly expensive single family homes, but a few choice apartments and houses for rent.

The weather in the Valley is what you'd expect. Summers are hottest in August & September when temperatures are in the high 90's and low 100's. High humidity occurs often with the intense heat. Summer is also peak smog season, usually producing daily unhealthy air (the stuff you can see before you breathe it). Occasional Santa Ana Winds blow the smog out to sea, creating cooler evenings and clearer skies. Fall is very pleasant, around mid 50's and Winter can be a cool 40.

Traveling from one side of the Valley to the other during rush hour normally takes 45 minutes to an hour. Traveling south to the beach can take the same amount of time on weekends, but double that time returning to the Valley (everyone seems to return home at the same time!).

The West Side

The hip, more chic communities of LA are on the West Side. These are West Hollywood, a predominantly gay community tucked into the Hollywood Hills with a wide variety of housing; Beverly Hills, the oo-la-la rich and famous playground where rents are exorbitant; West Los Angeles & Westwood, home to 20th Century Fox Studios, Fox-TV, Largo Entertainment and the ABC Entertainment Center, with housing catering to the students at the University of California at Los Angeles (UCLA), providing lots of housing opportunities; the Palms area, a bedroom community with affordable housing; the Fairfax district, home to CBS-Television City and plenty of affordable housing; and Brentwood, mostly expensive single family homes.

The weather on the West Side is generally 5-10 degrees cooler than the San Fernando Valley. Summers are hottest in August and September when temperatures are in the high 80's & low 90's. Humidity is not as bad as in the San Fernando Valley. Smog can appear in this area too (where doesn't it appear!). Just as with the San Fernando Valley, occasional Santa Ana Winds blow the smog out to sea and create cooler evenings and clear skies. Fall is very pleasant, around the mid 50's and Winter can be a cool 38. Travel time from Westwood to Universal Studios in the Valley can take 45 minutes to an hour.

The Beach Communities

If you are really and truly a beach person, then the beach communities are where you might want to look for housing. This area is made up of Malibu which has expensive housing with few rental opportunities; Santa Monica, a rent-controlled area with abundant housing; Venice, a mix of lower to moderately priced housing; and Culver City, home of Columbia Pictures,

Sony Pictures and MGM-UA with plenty of affordable housing. Then there are the beach communities referred to as the South Bay area: Marina Del Rey, expensive to moderately priced housing; Playa Del Rey, plenty of housing available; Manhattan Beach, Hermosa Beach, and Redondo Beach, all providing plenty of affordable housing.

The weather along the coast is generally 10 degrees cooler than the San Fernando Valley. Summers are hottest in August & September when temperatures are in the mid to high 80's. Smog can appear in this area too, but it's tough to spot. Just as in the San Fernando Valley, occasional Santa Ana Winds create cooler evenings and clearer skies. Fall is very pleasant, around the mid 50's and Winter can be a cool 38. From the beach to the San Fernando Valley normally takes an hour or more during rush hour.

There is one minor concern with living at the beach. Waking up every morning to the salt air, bright sun and beautiful sandy beach, it is too easy of a temptation to blow off work and play all day. If you're going to live at the beach, make sure you have the discipline to focus on your career, rather than on bathing suits!

San Gabriel Valley

East of and adjacent to the San Fernando Valley lies the San Gabriel Valley, a predominately single family housing area comprised of Pasadena, plenty of affordable housing; La Canada/ Flintridge, mostly expensive single family homes; La Crescenta, plenty of affordable housing; Montrose, plenty of affordable housing; Sierra Madre, Arcadia, and Monrovia, all bedroom communities with mostly single family homes and some rental apartments.

The weather in the San Gabriel Valley is hotter than that of the San Fernando Valley. Summers are hottest in August & September when temperatures are in the mid 100's. Humidity and smog are awful. It's not unusual for this region to experience 1st & 2nd Stage Smog Alerts daily in the Summer. Occasional Santa Ana Winds create cooler evenings and clearer skies, but it doesn't happen often. Fall is very pleasant, around mid 50's and Winter can be a cool 40.

Traveling from Pasadena to downtown LA takes about 30-45 minutes during rush hour. Traveling south to the beach can take an hour on weekends, but double the time returning.

Hollywood And Los Angeles

The center of this metropolitan area is Los Angeles. Its regions include Downtown LA, mostly artist's lofts at reasonable prices; Hollywood, home to Paramount Pictures, Raleigh Studios, Warner Brothers Hollywood and Sunset-Gower Studios, with plenty of affordable housing (though a bit of a seedy neighborhood) and nice old single family homes for rent in the Hollywood Hills; Hancock Park, old established neighborhood comprised of big old homes converted into affordable apartments; Park La Brea, mostly apartments; Silverlake, mostly older single family homes with some apartments; Mid-City, an ethnically diverse neighborhood with nice small single-family homes for rent; Echo Park, home of Dodger Stadium with an ethnically diverse community in lower to moderately priced housing; and Highland Park and Atwater Village, another ethnically diverse community with plenty of affordable housing.

The weather in this area is typical for the city. Summers are hottest in August & September when temperatures are in the high 80's. Humidity is a problem. Smog is apparent but is easily blown away by Santa Ana Winds. Fall is very pleasant, around mid 50's and Winter can be a cool 40. Traveling from Downtown LA to just about anywhere takes an hour. From Hollywood to the San Fernando Valley takes about 30 minutes during rush hour.

Even though apartment hunting is an arduous task, and in all probability will initially be done in the hottest part of the summer, it is still worth while to take your time and search for housing the right way the first time. It is absolutely too exhausting to do it twice.

APARTMENT EXPENSES AFTER MOVING IN

So now you have an apartment. You can grab your bags and move in, right? Wrong. There are still a number of things you'll need to take care of and a number of things you'll need to purchase before you move in.

Utility Service

The Department of Water and Power (DWP) provides both water and electricity which will cost around $50 for installation and roughly $30 to $50 per month. The Southern California Gas Company provides natural gas. It too will cost about $50 for installation and roughly $25-40 per month. See the appendix for DWP's phone number which can be called to activate service.

Refrigerator

It may be obvious, but you'll need a refrigerator. Most apartments come equipped with stoves or microwave ovens, but rarely do they come equipped with refrigerators. If you're living alone, you don't need a huge, state-of-the-art model. A small simple one will do. However, if you're sharing a place with one or more roommates, then you'll want to consider something a little bigger.

The best places in town to look for new refrigerators is at discount stores such as Circuit City. Generally, you can find refrigerators ranging in price from $100-800, depending on size and whether or not it is frost-free or has an icemaker. In addition, there is usually a delivery fee of about $30. But keep in mind, at these stores, the list price is *ALWAYS* negotiable.

Telephone Service

While you can buy a cheap phone almost anywhere for less than $25, setting up your phone service is a bit more expensive. Installation will run you about $40. This covers activation of the existing phone jacks in your house or apartment. If you wish to have additional phone jacks installed, the phone company will accommodate you at a cost of $75 for the first 15 minutes of work and $16 for each additional minute of work, so go very slow on this extra item if you're on a budget.

Flat monthly telephone service for an unlimited number of calls costs $11.25/month. Call Waiting adds another $3.50 per month and a one-time start-up cost of $5. Call Forwarding adds another $3.50 per month and a one-time start-up cost of $5. State & Federal taxes add up to about $7 per month. Therefore, your total monthly bill will be around $25 per month. Depending upon how many calls you make and to what part of Los Angeles those calls are directed, your monthly bill could be even higher, so go very slow on any extras until you need them. See the appendix for the phone number of the telephone company which you may call to activate your service.

In addition, you need to choose a long-distance carrier such as AT&T, MCI or Sprint. Depending upon how much you call, your long distance bill can be an additional $25-30/month or more.

The one additional investment, after you get settled and when you can afford the cost, is a good answering machine. Check Circuit City, Affordable Portables, Best Buys, or Good Guys discount audio stores for a deal on answering machines. The prices vary from $50-$350.

Pagers/Beepers

Later on, after you're established and also can afford it, you may also wish to obtain an answering service and/or a pager or beeper you can carry with you, although this is a service that should be delayed until you expect a lot of business calls. An answering service charges anywhere from $15-$35/month. A Pager costs roughly $90 to set-up the service, then a monthly fee of $15. I think the best beepers on the market are the Sky-Pagers from Skytel which allow you to go anywhere in the world and be paged. Pagers can be numeric (allowing only a phone number to be entered) or alpha-numeric (an operator types into a computer a message of any length and the whole message of words & numbers are displayed on the pager). Alpha-numeric pagers are very handy but do cost more per month (anywhere from $35-$65/month).

Now that you've settled into your apartment and have it up and running, take a breather, relax, enjoy yourself for a few days. The easy part is over. The tough part is about to begin - finding the first job!

THE BASICS

You've finally settled in Los Angeles. Congratulations and welcome! Now that the first leg of preparing for your new career is behind you, let's take a more detailed look at the specific "support" mechanisms that all beginning film careers share. This is the area that I call THE BASICS. Talent is one thing, but without developing these basics, the chances of having a successful career in "show biz" are slim.

THE RESUME

A universally important item, second only to the headshot for actors, is your resume. Type your resume on a typewriter, word processor or computer - it looks professional that way.

Don't use cheap paper; use 20-24 weight rag bond. It doesn't have to be fancy, but should be of good quality. A good resume can make a strong positive impression. A bad resume can keep you from ever getting an audition, interview or meeting. A poorly prepared resume will likely be thrown in the trash even if you have excellent qualifications. It is important to be professional at all times, and since your resume is your calling card, why not start presenting yourself professionally with a well prepared resume?

When making copies, make sure they look impressive. Cheap copies look like you were rushed and couldn't afford to invest in your career. Try using paper of muted color. A good choice might be a cream or off-white color.

Very important - don't forget to put your name on your resume. If it should become disconnected from your cover letter or headshot and it doesn't say your name, it's going to end up in the trash. That certainly would not help your employment chances.

Actors - cut your resume to fit your headshot. Since your headshot is usually 8" by 10", and standard bond paper is 8 1/2" by 11", you need to trim your paper to fit the headshot size. It looks cleaner and more professional this way. More about headshots later.

An important note about your resume: DON'T LIE! Belive me, you'll get caught.

What do you put on your resume? Here is a list of the **only** things you should put on your resume. They should be listed in roughly the following order:

- <u>Your Name</u> - no nicknames, unless you use a nickname professionally.

- <u>Agency Name</u> - if you have an agent, go ahead and list his name and telephone number.

- <u>Your Phone Number</u> - while you may list your home number, it is probably better to list a service number or pager number to protect you from being bothered at home by un-wanted phone calls.

- <u>Height, Weight, Hair Color, Eye Color</u> - this is only necessary for actors.

- <u>Film and TV Credits</u> - if you have any.

- <u>Stage Credits</u> - if you have any.

- <u>Special Skills</u> - if you have any.

- <u>Training & Education</u> - list your college degrees, but not dates. It often helps to indicate the names of selected instructors that may be recognizable to the entertainment industry - it may spark some interest in the reader if he is familiar with someone who instructed you.

- <u>Union Affiliations</u> - if you are a member of the Screen Actors Guild (SAG), Actors' Equity Association (AEA), American Federation of Television and

Radio Artists (AFTRA), American Guild of Variety Artists (AGVA), the Director's Guild of America (DGA), the Writer's Guild of America West(WGAw), or the International Alliance of Theatrical Stage Employees (IATSE), you should definitely indicate this.

And now here's what **should not** be on the resume.

- Age - in this industry, you can often be considered too young or too old. Better to keep them guessing. Actors should also refrain from listing their age range as it can limit you and keep you from being seen.

- Dates - again, keep them guessing and don't limit yourself.

- Social Security Number, Home Address, and Home Phone Number - it is too easy to find out personal and financial information about you and your family by listing this information. It is no one's business but your own. You can provide your Social Security number to your employer when you are given the job.

- Community Theater Credits - "Community" isn't the best of words; so try to emphasize the character or quality of the work: instead of saying Watertown Community Music Theater, say Watertown Music Theater. At this stage in the game, no one needs to know such minor details that suggest an amateur!

- the word "Resume" - using this word at the top of your resume may insult the reader's intelligence.

- nothing cute or autobiographical - be professional!

Display this information in an easy-to-read and organized fashion. An example of a good generic resume is illustrated in Figure 2. An example of an actor's resume can be found in the chapter entitled THE ACTOR.

Remember: DON'T LIE!

Film professionals will check your credits. Some of them may know individuals on some of the shows you are supposed to have been in. All they need to do is make a call and BANG! There goes the job prospects and a very good contact down the drain, as well as your reputation.

OTHER IMPORTANT TOOLS

Postage

Plan on spending money on postage for all those resumes and headshots you'll be sending out. Assuming you mail out 500 resumes and pictures in a year, at $0.55 per mailing, you'll be spending $275 a year alone in postage. Keep receipts for all your postage because you can often deduct the purchases as a business expense on your tax returns.

MICHAEL * ROSTKER

333 N Screenland Dr. #215, Burbank, CA 91505
phone: (818) 842-7523 *pager:* 1-800-508-7637 *email:* mrostker@earthlink.net

EXPERIENCE			
1997–98	Asst. to Manager for Quality Control	Studio Services Division	The Four Media Company
1997	Production Assistant	*Judge Judy*	Big Ticket Entertainment
	Production Assistant	*Buffalo Soldiers*	Citadel Entertainment
	Production Assistant	*Real Stories of the Donut Men*	Glazed Productions
	Asst. Lighting Designer	Various Projects (industrial)	The Tetlow Company, Inc.
	Asst. Lighting Designer	*Playback*	The Court Theatre
1996	Master Electrician	*Bedfellows*	The Skylight Theatre
	Lighting Designer	*Towards Canaan*	The Dorie Theatre
1995	Master Electrician	Summer Session	Struthers Library Theatre Playhouse
	Master Electrician	*The Cherry Orchard/Stars in the Morning Sky* (in rep.)	The Kresge Theatre
	Lighting Designer	*Curse of the Starving Class*	The CMU Studio Theatre
1994	Assistant Designer	Permanent Exhibit *How Things Fly*	National Air & Space Museum, Smithsonian Institution
	Lighting Designer	*Playing With Fire*	The CMU Studio Theatre
	Lighting Designer	*Abingdon Square*	The CMU Studio Theatre

ADDITIONAL SKILLS

Avid: Training on Avid Film/Media Composer. Completed the Avid 'bootcamp', a extensive series of classroom and hands-on training courses. Over 90 hours of classroom training included the survival class for assistant editors, advanced techniques, and troubleshooting for the Media Composer.

Computers: Extensive experience with Macintosh computers. Training in Pascal, C++ and HTML. Experience with UNIX and Windows. Some applications I have worked with:
- Microsoft: Word, Excel, Powerpoint
- Adobe: Photoshop, PageMaker, PageMill, Illustrator
- MiniCad+, AutoCad, form•Z, Lightwright, Filemaker Pro

Theatre: Experience with computer and manual lighting boards. Stage rigging in both hemp and counterweight houses.

Photography: Ability to process and print black & white photographs.

EDUCATION

Video Symphony, Burbank, CA. Avid 'bootcamp' including assistant editor survival course.

Carnegie Mellon University, Pittsburgh, PA. BFA in Drama.

EXAMPLE OF A GENERIC RESUME

FIGURE 2

Envelopes

You'll need these to send your resumes and pictures. This will cost you around $50.00 and should last you the year.

Answering Service/Answering Machine

Imagine Steven Spielberg's Producer calling your home to invite you to audition for a role in a new Dreamworks SKG film. But you've gone out grocery shopping and the Producer gets only a ringing on your end of the line. He'll hang up eventually, and may never call you again. You come home an hour later, with an armload of groceries, and never know just what an opportunity you missed. Now if you had an answering machine or an answering service, you would be at Dreamworks SKG right now.

Appointment Book/Calendar

This time, Martin Scorsese's Casting Director calls and he gets your answering machine (took my advice, did you?). He leaves a message about a role that he believes you will be absolutely perfect for, or about a production assistant job that is available, and tells you to appear at the studio on Monday. You come home an hour later, get the message, scream at the top of your lungs with excitement, erase the message from your machine and go on with the rest of your day.

Tuesday morning, you awake to an angry phone call from your agent - you missed your appointment with Scorsese's Casting Director yesterday! Where were you? Now if you had written the appointment down in an appointment book or calendar you would have made the appointment and might be starring in or working on the movie right now.

Index Card File

It's very important to keep track of *everyone* you meet. A handy way to accomplish this is to create a file of their names. Believe me; this industry is not very big, and you're bound to come across the same people time and time again.

The best system to use, other than a computer database, is a simple 3" x 5" note card file. On your cards, include as much information about each person as you can, and update the card as the information changes. For example, if you were making notes about a Casting Director, you would want to include on the card the following information:

- the person's name

- their address, phone numbers, and e-mail address

- the date of your last call/correspondence with them

- did you meet them or just send a mailing to them?

- did they bring you in for an audition or appointment?

- did they offer you a job?

- did you send them a thank you note?

- do they bring you in on a regular basis?

Stationary

This is another area where you can demonstrate your professionalism. Using quality stationary suggests that you have invested in your career. Writing a note to a producer, director or casting director on a sheet of paper from a legal pad or notebook will definitely not impress them. The better the stationary, the more likely you will be to get responses to your inquiries. Make the investment in your career!

Thank You Notes

Sometimes sending a thank you note for your appointment makes the difference between relative obscurity and consistent calls for appointments. Don't you like to be thought of and thanked occasionally? Well, so do others. Believe me; they'll remember you.

Theater, Showcases , Student Films & Classes

Just because you're looking for work doesn't mean you stop living. The best thing you can do is continue to participate in as much theater, film and classes as possible. Consider working for free on independent or student films as a grip, production assistant, or wardrobe assistant, to name but a few job opportunities. You may even wish to take a class or two to further educate yourself in areas with which you are less familiar such as electronic editing on an Avid Machine, or film scheduling and budgeting. Don't stop taking classes. Not only do you keep developing your craft, but you meet people who may recommend you for jobs and auditions. NETWORK! It's **so** important! In case you are wondering what networking is, it's what used to be called making, keeping and using "contacts." More about this later.

Postcards

As you begin to work on plays, films, and television, it is important to tell everyone about your success. Rather than sending out resumes, which can get expensive, try sending out 5" x 7" announcement postcards. On the front of the card, print an image (your headshot if you're an actor, a still photograph from your film if you're a director) that represents your craft or the project on which you're working. On the back of the card, print the key information about your latest endeavor and how you can be reached for more information about the project. You can use the postcard to invite agents, producers, studio executives and casting directors to watch your work, or use it to just touch base with a contact with whom you haven't worked in a while. Figure 3 illustrates an example of a good postcard.

Trade Subscriptions

While it is important to look in "The Trades" for jobs and auditions, it is just as important to stay on top of the latest happenings in the industry. The best sources for this information are the following "Trade" papers: *The Daily Variety, The Hollywood Reporter,* and *Backstage West/Dramalogue.*

Typewriter/Computer/Word Processor

If you cannot afford a word processor or computer, then you'll have to purchase a typewriter so you can keep your resumes up to date and maintain communication with the film community through type-written correspondence. Hand-written announcements, resumes, postcards, and other correspondence just doesn't cut it! More about computers and word processors later.

DEBORAH RIECKS
Amsel, Eisenstadt & Frazier
(213) 939-1188
Ric Beddingfield Mgt.
(310) 823-4004

DEBORAH RIECKS

Starring in the U.S. Premiere of
WUTHERING HEIGHTS

CRITIC'S CHOICE*
Riecks "smolders" – LA Times
"Riecks is a Scarlett O'Hara-esque beauty, instantly
believable as the manipulative and charming
Catherine" - LA Reader*

August 5 through October 8
Saturday 8pm o Sunday 5pm
The Knightsbridge Theatre
35 S. Raymond o Old Towne Pasadena
Industry Comps: (818) 972-6500

EXAMPLE OF A GENERIC POSTCARD

FIGURE 3

Videocassettes

How important is it to have some of your work on tape? ***Very important*** (which is why you'll need to spend money on transferring your work to videotape). For actors, it is the best example of your work for casting directors and film directors to see. It is also valuable for showing your work as a director, production designer, director of photography, lighting designer, etc. Everyone you meet will ask you, "What do you have on tape?"

NETWORKING

Half the battle of being a success in this business is having talent. The other half is having contacts. And those contacts can be developed by constantly networking. Very few of us will have the luxury of succeeding in this business because of nepotism, so we have to use whatever tools and skills we have to make it. Networking is one of the strongest of those tools. In fact, it may be *the* most important tool. If you have the right attitude about networking and learn how to do it successfully, you'll create more opportunities for yourself than any of your colleagues.

Networking is the art of using contacts to help you get what you want. For example, a Creative Producer may have a screenplay that he believes is exactly what a Creative Executive (CE) at a particular studio is looking for, but he may not know the CE personally. So he starts networking, asking his friends if any of them know the CE. But he strikes out. Then he goes to a party where he is introduced to a young woman whose brother is a film distribution executive. The brother also happens to be a good friend of the CE that the Creative Producer is interested in meeting. Instantly, the creative producer pitches his screenplay to the young woman, who likes the idea. The Creative Producer asks her for an introduction to her brother which she sets up. The Creative Producer then meets the brother and pitches the story to him. The brother likes it. The Creative Producer tells the brother that he thinks the screenplay is right up the alley of the CE and asks the brother for an introduction. The brother sets it up, the Creative Producer pitches to the CE who loves the story, and a sale is made. Yes, I agree it is an overly simplistic story of networking success, but it does demonstrate my point.

The same technique, in varying forms, can be used by actors, writers, directors, virtually anyone in the film business who has something to sell - themselves! Networking is *the key* to success. As they say, "it's who you know." So now that you know you must network to succeed, let's talk about a few things you can do to start the networking ball rolling.

Coaching Groups

As you start working on your career, you're bound to meet many others out there trying to do the same thing. Why not pool your resources together and help one another by creating Coaching Groups? Gather a group of five to ten individuals seeking employment in the industry and, together, establish a weekly meeting where you will all convene faithfully, without missing one session, where you can begin a networking group. Each member of the group should have his or her own goal: to appear in feature film, to sell a screenplay, to be offered an editing job on a television show, etc. The goals should be realistic and attainable. For example, a man who has never taken an acting class, never been in a play, never acted in his life, should not make as his initial goal "to star in a feature motion picture." The chances of that happening are one in a million. Be realistic.

The idea behind a coaching group is to be accountable to one another for each other's success. Jim is accountable to Bob for Bob's success. Bob is accountable to Jim for Jim's success. Jim is also accountable to Sue for Sue's success, and so on. You're all in this together to get what you want and to help the others get what they want. Throw out selfishness: be just as committed to the success of the other group members as you are to your own.

Each week, members of the group should take a few minutes to describe what they accomplished that week towards reaching their goal. After each person is done talking, everyone else in the group should begin to throw out ideas about what to do next that the individual may not have considered. Don't hold back your ideas even if you think they're silly. I've seen the most ridiculous ideas work! You'll find that people in the group will know people you haven't contacted yet and may help provide an introduction for you.

Continue this every week, faithfully, until each person in the group has reached their goal. Somewhere along the line, a member of the group may decide his goal may not be realistic and wish to change to another goal. That's okay. Just keep working to move forward. The idea is not only to succeed at the immediate task, but to keep building a larger and stronger network so that, if you accomplish your first goal, the next goal will have a larger network available to it.

If networking is not one of your strong suits, or you just don't know where to start with networking, I'd strongly suggest taking a course to develop your networking skills. One of the best courses I can recommend is a 4-week class called "Flash Forward," founded by Suzanne Lyons & Heidi Wall. Classes are made up of a maximum of 50 people all in the same boat as you - they want to start networking. Some of the people who take the class have been working in the business for years, but are just not confident in their networking skills. Others are new to the business of networking. Together, the class members coach and encourage one another to take risks while learning to recognize networking opportunities, how to make telephone calls to people you don't know to seek information, advice and guidance, how to "work a room," how to make a meeting a successful networking experience, etc.

The class meets one evening a week. The course costs $345.00 but is well worth the investment (I am an alumnus of the course). If you're interested in finding out more about the class and other courses available through the Flash Forward Institute, write to the following address (or call), and you will receive information through the mail:

Flash Forward
235 N. Valley Street, Suite 328
Burbank, CA 91505-3941
(818) 558-1890
(818) 842-4112 Fax

GETTING AN AGENT

It's tough in this town to get a job as an actor, writer, director or producer without an agent. While technically, you don't need an agent, you're probably better off with one than without one. While opinions may vary about agents, there is no question that they have their purpose and place in our industry. So, what does an agent do?

The Writer's Agent

An agent representing a writer is responsible for getting the writer's script read by people who can either purchase the script or who can be influential in the eventual purchase of the script. When a party offers to purchase a script, the writer's agent is responsible for negotiating, on the writer's behalf, the best possible contract including the purchase price. In a nutshell, the agent is responsible for telling everyone who will listen (and some who won't) that the writer is the next up-and-coming Steve Zaillian and they would be lucky to get their hands on him first.

The Director's Agent

A director's agent is responsible for looking over the screenplays, which have been written by writers represented by the same agency, that are in development at various production companies and/or studios. The agent then submits the director's name as a potential director if one has not already been attached to the screenplay. If the director has an idea for a screenplay, the agent is responsible for getting the director a meeting with studio executives and/or producers to whom he can pitch the story. The agent should view the director as the next Spike Lee, and should be telling everyone who will listen that they don't want to pass him up.

The Producer's Agent

A producer's agent's job is to look over the screenplays that the clients of the agency currently have in development at various production companies and/or studios, and submit the producer's name as a potential producer if one is not already attached to the screenplay. If the producer has an idea for a screenplay, the agent is responsible for getting him meetings with studio executives and/or investors to whom he can pitch the story. In a nutshell, the agent should be spreading the word around town that he handles the next Jerry Bruckheimer, and that this producer has screenplays that may be of interest.

The Actor's Agent

In the film business, the one agent that is probably the most well-known is the actor's agent - simply because everyone wants to be a star (some even believe they already are!). As such, this agent is doing his job if he is getting an actor an audition. He does this by looking over the cast breakdowns that come in to his office each day to see if any of his clients fit any of the available parts. Cast breakdowns are created by companies who distribute information about films currently being cast and, describe in great detail, the roles that are available. This information is submitted to them by casting directors. If an agent feels his client is right for any of the parts listed in the breakdown, he then submits the actor's picture and resume to the appropriate casting director and begins to sell the actor to the casting director.

The Artist's Commitment

Although you've agreed to be represented by an agent, and are expecting him to be out there selling you to the industry, don't think your job is over. You have to hustle as well. After you've completed a screenplay and turned a copy over to your agent, or after you've completed your audition, or finished your pitch to a studio executive, don't think you can sit back and wait until the money rolls in. On the contrary, your agent will expect you to hustle as much as he does.

The Agent's Reward

In exchange for his work, an agent takes 10% of the monies received from his client's employment. He also takes 10% of any additional monies received from his client's share of the box office profits and other ancillary markets (foreign box office, videocassettes, merchandising, etc.).

Getting An Agent

How do you get an agent? Well, the first thing you should know is not to sign with an agent unless he is a _franchised agent._ A franchised agent has agreed in writing with the various unions (WGAw, SAG, and DGA) to abide by all union regulations. You can contact each union for a list of their franchised agents.

A sure way of knowing if an agent is not on the up-and-up is if he asks you for money. Regardless of what it's for, the minute he asks, start running and don't look back. He's probably a crook and you can bet he's not a franchised agent.

There are a number of ways to find an agent. You can do a letter writing campaign to every agent for whom you can find an address, remembering to include a synopsis of your script or a headshot and resume. There are a number of resource guides which list agencies that are available at a variety of bookstores in Los Angeles. Check the Appendix for the addresses and phone numbers of a few.

From these mailings, you'll be lucky if you get two or three responses. But don't wait for them to call you; pick up the phone and call them *one week* after you've mailed your letters. Introduce yourself to the assistant who answers the phone and tell that person that you have mailed the agent a letter with a script synopsis or a headshot/resume because you are seeking representation. You would like to know if the agency is currently looking to add more clients and if so, you would like an interview. While 9 times out of 10 they'll say they aren't seeing anyone, don't be annoyed or disappointed. Simply thank them and hang up - then plan to call them again in three to four weeks and repeat the process. This same thing could go on for many weeks, maybe months. But sooner or later, they'll respond to your persistence and you'll get your meeting. Remember to be nice to the agent's assistant. This person is a future agent and the last thing you want to do when starting out is make an enemy of "the little people".

The best way, however, to find an agent is to talk to colleagues about their agents. You will develop plenty of colleagues once you settle in. Ask your colleagues which agents represent them and whether or not they are happy with them. If they are, ask them if they would be willing to introduce you to their agent, and even put in a good word for you with the agent. Then send your letter, script synopsis, resume, or headshot to the agent and ask for a general interview. If one of your stage plays is running at a local theater, or a student film you've written, directed or starred in is screening, send the agent a postcard inviting him to watch the production or film. An example of what to write on a postcard can be found in Figure 4.

Choosing an Agent

When it comes to choosing the right agent, you can help yourself by doing some preliminary research. When you meet him, check him out:

- Clout - an agent with clout is going to open more doors. Some studio executives won't take calls from unknown agents or agents who are known to represent unknown talent. By reading the trade papers and keeping track of the agencies and agent names mentioned in them, you can start to get a sense of which agencies, and specifically which agents, are getting their clients work. If they're getting their clients work, then it means the agent is getting in the door. If he's getting in the door, he's developing his clout. Short of this, ask around and you'll learn who can and who can't open doors.

- Offices and Employees - what do his office and his employees look like? Disorganized and unkempt is a sure-fire sign that it's time to move on.

- Enthusiasm - does he have enthusiasm for you and for the industry? If so, that's a positive. But if he's constantly complaining about the business, and he comes across uncertain about your potential, move on to someone else.

Dear Mr. Makeastar,

You and a guest are cordially invited to the upcoming production of "Making a Star" at The Court Theater in which I play the lead character of "James." The Court Theater is located at 722 North La Cienega Blvd. in Hollywood. We open on Friday September 13th and close on Friday December 24th. Performances are on Thursday, Friday, and Saturday evenings at 8:00pm.

Please call me at 818-555-1000 to make a reservation to insure that two good seats will be held for you.

Please join us for what I am certain will be a thoroughly enjoyable evening.

Sincerely,

Ima Star

Mr. Makestar
Bigtime Productions
100 Anywhere St.
Los Angeles, CA 90038

EXAMPLE OF A POSTCARD TO AN AGENT

FIGURE 4

- <u>Agency Size</u> - you may want to get into a small or mid-size agency, rather than the giants like CAA, ICM and William Morris when first starting out. You don't want to be a forgotten little fish in a big pond.

- <u>How Many Clients Does He Handle?</u> - no agent can handle more than 25 clients himself. Ask him how many clients he represents. If he has more than 25, move on.

- <u>How Does He See You?</u> - if you and he are on different wavelengths about where your market is, one of you needs to take a second look. Make sure it's not your ego talking. Also, if you are writing or developing screenplays, see what kind of stories he wants you to write or develop - if they're different than the type of stories that interest you, move on.

- <u>How Often Does He Want to Be Contacted?</u> - good agents want to hear from you often.

- <u>How Much Work Does He Expect You to Do on Your Own?</u> - if you get the feeling that this is a one-sided issue, maybe you should find someone a little more interested in doing his job.

<u>You and Your Agent: A Partnership</u>

So, now you have an agent. Don't expect the job offers to start flowing in. As in any other career, you need to work at finding a job. That's the responsibility of the agent, you say. If that was entirely true, you could sit home watching television until the call for a job comes. But it doesn't work that way. You have to look for job opportunities just as much as your agent does. Think of it as a partnership. It's like riding a tandem bicycle, and each of you has to pedal. If only one person does his share of the work, the bicycle slows down and goes nowhere. But if you both pull your weight, you could really go places!

So, how do you motivate the partnership? Here are some general guidelines about things you can do to keep up your end of the agreement:

- keep his office stocked with copies of your screenplays, resumes and head shots. How else is he "gonna get your name around town?"

- look for work on your own by networking and knocking on any doors that are suggested to you by others.

- be active and visible - don't just sit at home waiting for the phone to ring, get out and create opportunities such as appearing in local plays or having your own plays produced in local theaters, responding to "screenplays wanted" listings in Dramalogue, etc.

- as a writer, producer or director, keep practicing your pitching technique; be prepared to pitch at a moment's notice.

- be on time and don't miss meetings.

- be reachable - do answering machines, answering services and beepers ring a bell? If not, go back and read about the things you need when you first arrive in LA in the "Moving to Los Angeles" Section.

- network, network, network! Attend as many parties, meetings, screenings, any function where you know film industry people will appear and "work the room" by introducing yourself to people. By meeting new people, you're bound to find someone who will help you get an audition, or listen to a quick pitch and maybe even read your script.

- keep in touch

Now you know what your agent will expect of you. So, let's take a look at what a good agent can do to fulfill his part of the agreement:

- consistently submits you and talks about you - if he's not doing this, he shouldn't be an agent.

- tells you the truth - if you can't trust your agent, dump him.

- represents you well and negotiates for you in good faith.

- keeps an office that is decent and organized - if he's a mess here, just think what kind of submission he does with your screenplay.

- returns your calls and inquiries - as long as you're not bugging him.

- follows up on your suggestions.

- shows interest in you and sees/reads your work - how else is he going to know what you can and cannot do?

Just meeting these requirements is not enough. We know the agent only makes money if he closes a deal for you. But he also represents other talent, some of whom may be working more than you. He's more apt to focus on them than on you since they're the ones who are currently providing him with an income.

How do you keep him interested in you? By building a strong relationship with him. For example, after being with your agent for a while, take him to lunch or dinner and talk about other things than your career. Get to know one another on a level other than business. Work to make a colleague of him.

And don't forget to thank your agent with a "thank-you" note for getting you an audition or interview. Agents have feelings too, believe it or not, and they truly appreciate being thanked because so few people ever stop to do so.

THE RIGHT FRAME OF MIND

The basics which we have just covered, standing alone, will not guarantee you success, but you can't even get close without them. Right along side this, and something I believe is truly more valuable, is having the right frame of mind about your career. It can make all the difference. Here are some examples of what I mean:

- Define your type, your market: this requires putting your ego in check. I know a multitude of aspiring actors who desperately want to be leading men, but just don't have the "right look." I tell them time and again that they should be representing themselves as character actors, and yet they continue to go out for leading men calls. You'd think they would figure it out when they don't get cast as leading men. It's humbling to recognize that you won't get cast the way you want. But if you want to be a working actor, then be honest with yourself and think intelligently about your type. And just what is the "right look?" It's that indescribable "it." When a casting director and/or director see "it," they know "it."

  The same holds true for writers, directors and producers. If you're not funny, don't write comedy. If you're funny but not emotional, don't write drama. If you aren't comfortable giving actors emotional direction, then stick to directing action films instead of period dramas. Know what your strengths are and how the market perceives these strengths. Chances are that's where you'll find most of your employment.

- <u>Know your craft</u>: don't stop taking classes. Good industry professionals take classes for the rest of their lives, learning, exploring, honing their skills. There's always something to learn. UCLA and the American Film Institute (AFI) both offer extension courses in a variety of areas including film scheduling and budgeting, film editing techniques, advanced acting, dialects, and improvisation, etc., for a nominal fee.

- <u>Get off your own back</u>: everyone makes mistakes. Don't be too hard on yourself if you screw up an audition or flub a line here or there. Remember, it's not brain surgery!

- <u>Be professional</u>: don't put up with non-professionals. I don't mean be arrogant, but if someone is rude to you, don't sit there and take it because you need the work and you're afraid they'll never hire you. Don't be afraid to stand up for what you believe in, but be professional about it.

- <u>Don't need the money</u>: stash some money away so that you can walk away when you choose to. If you "need the money," you'll look too desperate for work and someone may end up taking advantage of you.

- <u>Don't hang-out with complaining, non-working professionals</u>: they're too negative, and they'll drag you down. Negativity spreads like a bad case of cancer. Get into a coaching group instead.

- Always act successful: I don't mean cocky, but know your value in your field. Looking successful and having a successful attitude always impresses people.

- Always be positive: so your car broke down this morning; you're overdrawn on your checking account; you lost a job to a real yo-yo. Doesn't matter - be positive. Don't let the interviewer know that things are bothering you. Be up; be happy; don't let things get you down. Remember, enthusiasm sells.

UNIONS

Los Angeles is a union town. There are so many unions and locals in this town that you can't count them on your hands...or your feet, for that matter. Unions have been described as both a blessing and a curse. While there are definite benefits to becoming a union member, once you have joined a union, non-union work is no longer allowed. Union members occasionally perform non-union work, but they run the risk of losing their union membership *forever* if they get caught. A great deal of the work in Los Angeles is non-union, but the bigger budgeted, higher profile projects are all union. So who are the unions? The most important unions are:

- Director's Guild of America (DGA) which represents directors, unit production managers and assistant directors in motion pictures and television

- <u>Writer's Guild of America</u> (WGA) which represents writers in motion pictures and television. There are separate offices on both the East and West coasts, commonly refered to as WGAw and WGAe

- <u>Screen Actors Guild</u> (SAG) which represents actors and background extras in motion pictures

- <u>American Federation of Television and Radio Artists</u> (AFTRA) which represents radio performers as well as actors in live and taped television and commercials

- <u>Actors' Equity Association</u> (AEA) often referred to as "Equity," which governs actors and stage managers in the theater

- <u>American Guild of Variety Artists</u> (AGVA) represents singers, magicians, clowns, stand-up comics, nightclub performers and circus performers

- <u>American Guild of Musical Artists</u> (AGMA) represents classical singers, dancers, soloists, choral singers, opera singers, etc.

- <u>International Alliance of Theatrical Stage Employees</u> (IATSE or IA) is the international brotherhood representing the 30 or more IATSE and Basic Craft Offices in the motion picture and television industry. For each specific industry labor craft, electricians for example, there is a Local. A Local is an office in a specific city which has been granted an IATSE Charter allowing the Local to represent and induct union members in their jurisdiction. This means that there may be an Electricians Local in Los Angeles, as well as in New York City, Chicago, Cleveland, etc. The IATSE Union Locals in Los Angeles are:

Local 44	Property Craftsmen
Local 80	Studio Grips
Local 468	Studio Mechanics
Local 600	International Photographers
Local 683	Film Technicians
Local 695	International Sound Technicians
Local 695P	Studio Projectionists
Local 705	Costumers
Local 706	Make-up Artists & Hair Stylists
Local 727	Crafts Service
Local 728	Studio Electrical Lighting Technicians
Local 729	Set Painters
Local 767	Studio First Aid Employees
Local 776	Film Editors
Local 790	Illustrators & Matte Artists
Local 816	Scenic Artists
Local 818	Publicists
Local 839	Screen Cartoonists
Local 847	Set Designers & Model Makers
Local 854	Story Analysts
Local 871	Script Supervisors
Local 876	Art Directors
Local 884	Studio Teachers & Welfare Workers
Local 892	Costume Designers

The Basic Craft Offices are comprised of five Locals which have agreed to negotiate as a collective group with regard to working conditions, rates and fringe benefits. The Basic Craft Offices in Los Angeles are:

Local 40	Electrical Workers (IBEW)
Local 78	Plumbers
Local 399	Transportation Drivers (Teamsters)
Local 399	Location Managers
Local 724	Studio Utility Employees
Local 755	Ornamental Plasterers and Cement Masons

Each union has its own unique set of regulations and working conditions. They each also have their own set of requirements for membership. I discuss the specifics of these requirements in the individual sections for each of The Players.

THE SECOND JOB

We've been talking about getting a "reel" job, but it really is the second job that will keep you alive until the Big Break arrives. Be smart about finding a part-time job. You need something that provides flexible hours, allows you time to go out on interviews and auditions, and still allows you time to take classes. You want to find a job that gets you talking to and working with industry people. If they like you, they'll help you. **REMEMBER: THIS IS A BUSINESS AND YOU ARE IN THE SALES DEPARTMENT - SELL YOURSELF!!** Let's take a look at one of the best second jobs available to the beginning film professional.

Temporary Services Work

Although it may not seem to be a suitable employment alternative for you, temporary services work is actually one of the best "foot-in-the-door" opportunities to consider when first looking for work. Often referred to as "temp work", temporary services is just what it sounds like: providing a company a service on a short-term or temporary basis.

The temporary work industry began back in the seventies and grew rapidly during the last two decades. You may be familiar with the names of two of the earliest and biggest, Manpower and Kelly Services (originally Kelly Girl). The industry has grown so much that many of these temp agencies now specialize in certain types of employees and services, the biggest by far being office and clerical, which includes computer related skills. At Disney, for example, temps are often hired from The Right Connection, Our Gang, or Apple One, just three of the many temp respected agencies in business.

As an example of temp work, let's say that the assistant to a Creative Executive at Warner Brothers Studios has unfortunately come down ill with the flu and cannot go into work. Rather than fend for himself, the Creative Executive contacts his Human Resources Department (HR) and orders a "temp". This means that the HR person will contact a temporary services company in order to hire a skilled assistant for the day to cover for the sick employee. This temporary assistant will provide the Creative Executive with the same basic assistance that the executive's full-time assistant would normally do were he on the job and not home sick.

Working as a temp is an excellent way to get your foot in the door inside the decision-making offices of the executives, producers, directors, and writers who run the film and television industry. It's a great way to network with people, find out who is working with whom, observe the decision-making process inside the industry, and potentially, find that elusive "first job". Temp work is great for actors who need a flexible schedule in order to be available for auditions on a moment's notice.

The Necessary Skills

Not everyone can be a temp. Only those who can master certain specific skills will be employed as temps. Although I've never actually worked as a temp, I do know a number of people who have. A few of them have been kind enough to share some of their experiences and knowledge about the world of temp work.

Marisa, a colleague of mine who works for a major studio ordering temps on an as-needed basis, says that temp work is a great entry into the film industry. "Nine times out of ten, you will be asked to do every-day kinds of tasks such as answering phones, taking messages, making copies, sending faxes, distributing mail, accepting deliveries, and functioning as a receptionist." She stresses that in the high-pressure world of motion pictures, executives don't have the time to teach you these things. Indeed, if you have to be taught these things on the job, you won't last long as a temp, and the agency that recommended you won't be getting much work from that client again. In addition, you will need a certain level of proficiency in the skills usually needed in office work.

Probably the most useful skill requirement is typing. You don't have to be in the Guiness Book of World Records for typing, but you should be able to handle at least 30 words per minute, preferably more. The Right Connection, a leading temp agency here in Los Angeles, requires that a temp be able to type a minimum of 30 words per minute to be accepted into their pool of temps. The more words per minute you can type, the better chance you have of getting work. It doesn't matter if you are a two-finger typist or a pro, the bottom line is how proficient you are.

In this day and age of personal computers, you'll also need a fairly high degree of familiarity with many of the more popular software programs and with computer systems, The Right Connection stresses that if you do not have competent computer skills, you will not find work as a temp. They require that a prospective temp be conversant with *at least* Word For Windows™, Microsoft Excel™, and Microsoft Word™ for Mac computers. They encourage you to be conversant in more than just these three, but without knowledge of these three, your chances of being hired by The Right Connection are dramatically reduced. You may have your own personal preference when it comes to a word processing program, but the company you are temping for may prefer another program. If you don't know their preferred program, you won't get the work.

The film industry uses a variety of different software programs. The more conversant you are with them, the more valuable a temp you become. Some of the more popular and frequently used software programs in the film industry are FileMaker Pro™, Microsoft PowerPoint™, Adobe PageMaker™, Now Up-To-Date™, Lotus 1-2-3™, Calendar Creator™, Calendar Maker™, Adobe Photoshop™, Final Draft™, Movie Magic Scheduling™, Movie Magic Budgeting™, and Movie Magic Screenwriter™.

When I spoke with The Right Connection, they stressed the importance of knowing Mac, IBM-compatible, and Windows computer systems. Most types of office software are available for both systems, however, they may have slight differences in the way they function on the respective systems.

Interestingly enough, you don't have to have a film background in order to find work with an entertainment temp agency. Apple One, one of the temp agencies that Disney uses, says that it is more important that you are computer literate and at least 18 years of age than have a degree in film. "As long as you're 18, you know computers, and you have a desire to work in the film industry, we'll consider you," one of the Apple One Placement Representatives told me. Even if you've graduated from one of the highly respected university films schools such as UCLA, USC, or NYU, if you don't know computers, you won't get hired as a temp.

While it is of great importance to have these basic office skills, it is perhaps of greater importance that you understand the psychology of the situation you will be in. Each of the three parties involved really have different goals and you don't want to be in conflict with those of the other two. *You* are trying to earn a living while trying to get a break in the entertainment industry. *The temp agency* wants to earn a profit on your labor and impress the client company so as to get more business. *The client company* simply wants the office chores done, and done right. The temp agency may be sympathetic to your career goals, but they want first and foremost for you to do the temp job in an impressive manner.

So don't get confused about why you're there. Get the exposure to the industry, meet the people, but get the job done.

Contacting Temporary Services Agencies

Once you feel confident in your basic office skills, you can prepare yourself for contacting the many temp agencies about employment opportunities. The best way to make your initial introduction to the agency is by mailing them a cover letter and resume. Later in this book, in the chapter entitled FILM TECH-NICIANS, I explain what makes a good cover letter. You can use the same principles here when preparing your cover letter.

Earlier in this chapter, I discussed what makes a good resume. Again, use the same principles here when developing your resume. In addition, I want to point out a few specific things that relate directly to the temp business that will influence the way you set up your resume for temp work:

- <u>Be professional</u> - type your resume on paper of reasonable quality. Go back and read the paragraphs on preparing a resume at the beginning of this section.

- <u>Be thorough and accurate</u> - all the information about yourself should be error-free: names, addresses, telephone numbers, dates, references, etc.

- <u>Don't lie and don't exaggerate</u> - if you claim skills at which you are not proficient, you will disappoint the client, and you will be a failure in the eyes of the temp agency. Word will get around: end of a possibly profitable temp career.

- <u>Spelling and grammar</u> - check and double check every word, every punctuation mark, and every sentence. Nothing is more certain to "deep-six" your chances for a job than sloppy writing.

- <u>Reference</u> - you may be too new to Los Angeles to have local references, but no matter. Give references from home, college, or the last job. Any reference is better than no reference. *And,* you can be sure that the references will be checked.

One of the best ways to insure that your letter will be read by the managers of the agency is to include in your cover letter a referral. If a relative or colleague has worked with the temp agency before and would be willing to recommend you, use this information in your letter. In fact, when I recently called The Right Connection, the Placement Represetative I spoke to said to me, "If you have someone that you think would make a good temp, when they call us for an interview, make sure they use your name and we'll get them in right away for an interview." Good recommendations are a decided advantage and may help you to get an interview with the agency. *Remember: do not lie.* Don't use someone's name as a referral if you have not asked them first. Lying will be uncovered, I can assure you, and eliminate any possible chance of work as a temp.

Once an agency has received your resume and reviewed it, they will contact you should they find that you are a suitable candidate. Some agencies do not call you if you do not meet the prerequisites they are looking for. If you do not hear from them, contact them and see if they did in fact receive your letter and resume. It may have been misplaced as they are constantly getting resumes, timecards, and all sorts of important documents sent to them.

The Interview

Temp Agencies receive lots and lots of resumes every week. Most have only certain times when they will meet prospective temps for interviews. For example, Apple One will meet with people from 8:00am to 11:00am and then again from 2:00pm to 4:00pm. So when the agency calls you to come in for an interview, understand their time constraints and work with them to schedule your appointment at a convenient time.

Like almost everything in the film industry, it's best to get an early start. In this instance, the same philospophy can be applied. I always try to schedule meetings as early as possible in the morning when I'm sure that the people I'm meeting with are awake, energized and ready to start the day. Towards the end of the day, people tend to be either sleepy and less attentive, or irritable and anxious to get out of the office. As such, if it's possible, try to schedule your interview early in the day.

There are some basic rules about interviews:

- always leave enough driving time so as to arrive early at your interview. This will indicate your eagerness to work and commitment to professionalism.

- from the moment you walk in the front door to the time you say goodbye, be professional and courteous. You've heard the expression "kill 'em with kindness." Live it!

- take enough time to fill out all forms and question-naires completely and free of errors. Remember the impact of first impressions!

- be smart about how you dress. Would you hire some-one who came to their interview dressed suggestively, in tennis shoes, or wearing jeans?

After completing all preliminary paperwork, you'll probably be asked to take a series of tests before you get to the interview itself. But don't get uptight if it seems that it takes forever for these things to happen. Remember, the agency's first concern is satisfying the client and you are just a means to that end. So always be patient and always smile.

The tests you'll be asked to take are designed to evaluate your office skills. Again, don't get uptight about these tests. If you didn't lie or over exaggerate about your abilities in your resume, then the tester knows generally what to expect and this phase of the process should go smoothly.

There are really only three types of tests given:

- A typing test. More than likely this test will be one using a computer or word processor and some type of word processing software. Here, accuracy may be more important than speed.

- Are you computer literate? This is more than just typing. Can you use the "standard" office software programs that their clients use? Can you open, close, save, delete, edit, work spreadsheets, and print?

- A basic skills test. The operative word here is "basic." Arithmetic, spelling, and grammar are the standard skills on which you will be tested. However, some agencies have been known to given you multiple choice, "what would you do in this situation" type questions.

If you have fudged your resume and can't really pass these tests, don't take the tests! Failure here stamps you as a poor future risk and the agency will probably not call you in again. Instead, call the agency, tell them you're a bit rusty on your skills and need a little more time to brush up. Ask them for suggestions of firms that provide quick brush-up courses in these skills. When you're ready, call them back. The agency will respect your honesty and effort.

When all of this is done, you will then be interviewed by agency personnel. Interview methods, styles and techniques vary considerably and are as much a matter of skill as the interviewer's personality. The one certainty is that no matter the interviewer's methods, one question will always remain in the interviewer's mind: do you fit the clients' needs? He'll find the answer by assessing the tests you took, the answers to the interview questions, and the resume you provided (remember to bring one along just in case he asks for a copy).

Acceptance In An Agency

Once the agency accepts you and tells you that they'll call you when they have an assignment, you then have additional important responsibilities:

- Provide the agency with your schedule of availability. You may want to exclude days when you're taking classes, appearing in a play, or attending a group help seminar. But, if you're going to be available on any given day, or for any given period of time, call the night before or early the next morning, and tell the agency. The night before or the early morning is often the time when the agency gets the client's call for help.

- At the same time, be sure to let the agency know if you're available for a long or short stay. If the client wants someone for a week and you go in planning to work only three days because of a scheduled film audition, a very embarrassing situation would arise.

When the call comes and you're ready, willing and anxious to work, you still have some key considerations:

- Ask about the location and the starting time before you accept the job. Most office jobs start at 8:00am, but some begin at 7:00am, and a few at 9:00am. So, commuting time and distance become a factor. Be absolutely certain you can make the long commute at rush hour and be on time for work before you accept.

- Ask about the specifics of the job and what you'll be expected to do, and at what skill level. If the job requires more than you know you can do, have the courage to turn it down and explain why. The agency will appreciate your honesty in avoiding an embarrassing situation, and you'll live to work some other day.

- If there is a fit and you accept, then be wise enough to get these important specifics: starting and finishing times; if overtime may be required; starting pay rate; the exact address; the telephone number in case you get lost; location of parking for temporary employees; who to ask for when you arrive; and the name of the person who will be your immediate supervisor if he is not the person who meets you.

- You dressed professionally when you interviewed with the temp agency. Do it again for the first day of work. Different companies have different dress codes, as well as different views of what "casual" means. You'll learn on the first day what is appropriate and acceptable,

• If the person who is your supervisor isn't going to be around much, or the nature of the job leaves you on your own, find out early who to turn to in case of problems or unexpected circumstances. For much the same reason, you will want to be polite and considerate of everyone you meet, particularly co-workers. They are people who can show you "the ropes" and make life a lot simpler. They can also make positive comments to the boss about your performance.

• Always have a positive attitude and smile. No one wants to work with a grouch. Thank people when they answer your questions and when they've helped you. People notice and appreciate kindness and consideration. Similarly, don't wait to be asked to help others. Offer to help anyone anytime you have a break in your own work load. People will remember, and good words will flow up to management.

If you find that the temp job you're performing is to your liking and you'd like to get called back when the need exists, then the first thing to do is *not* to approach your supervisor or the personnel department about future callbacks or permanent employment. That will quickly establish you as a person who came to them under false pretenses. And in that instance, chances are good that you'll not see that client again. If you want to be called back, then the way to do it is to impress them with the quality and quantity of your work, your professionalism, and your pleasant personality.

Other Second Jobs

Temporary services work is only one of a variety of second jobs available to you. Here are some suggestions on other possible jobs to look for:

- Waiting Tables: many of these jobs are available and they provide a good living. However, they can be tough and exhausting jobs. The better you are, the better the restaurant you'll work in. Do your job well. People notice that. Try to work in a place where industry types hang out, not just some dive that pays the rent.

- Secretarial: it's tough to find jobs where you're only required to work in the evenings, but they do exist. Good secretaries are worth their weight in gold. Many of the temp agencies provide work opportunities for secretaries so you may want to sign up with one of the numerous agencies. The key to finding secretarial work is having the required skills. So brush up on your typing and dictation skills. It is also a requirement to be computer knowledgeable, both Windows™ and Mac. The benefit of temp jobs is that you can pretty much set your own hours (i.e., three or four days a week, six to eight hours a day) and still allow yourself quality time for reading scripts, writing, meetings, and auditioning.

- Production Company "Gofer": this job gets you into the offices of a lot of studio executives, producers, directors and casting directors. Not a bad place to start, and you'll get to know all the back roads of

Los Angeles. This is a good networking job. However, if you're an actor, remember not to tell anyone at the production company that what you really want to do is act because you'll never be hired. The production company will think you'll be more interested in using their contacts to find acting work than in paying attention to the job at hand. If you're gong to do this type of work, concentrate on your assignments - if they're happy with you, they'll help you with other opportunities. This was my first job in the industry and it opened a tremendous number of doors for me.

- Assistant to a Casting Director: most casting directors won't hire actors as assistants, so don't tell them you want a career as an actor. However, this is a good networking job because you'll meet many producers and directors.

- Tele-Marketing: if you can sell ice to Eskimos, this job is for you. If you have a pleasant phone voice and can be very convincing over the telephone, you were made for this job. In general, you can set your own hours and often work only three or four days a week, while still bringing in $650-1000/week. And often, you can work this job at night.

- Chauffeurs: for this job, you must have a citation and accident-free record. You'll spend all day fighting the God-awful LA traffic, but you can make good money and work when you're available. In addition, you can set your own hours and be available only at night. Each driving assignment pays okay, but the tips can be great. Plus, you never know who you'll be driving around town - he might be a terrific industry contact. If you're good at this job, you'll be in demand and develop a regular clientele.

- Catering: many of my colleagues started out working as waiters for catering companies. The advantages are many:

    1) catering pays well

    2) the days and hours are flexible

    3) you generally work only at night allowing you the day to audition, take classes, go to pitch sessions, etc.

    4) you can often work industry parties where you'll meet loads of industry people with whom you can network

THE PLAYERS

You've recently graduated from college where the last four years have been spent focusing on "the craft, the techniques, and the art form." At school, they say to you, "take a chance, take a risk, be willing to fall flat on your face with grace." However, in the film industry, you are told you, "if you take a chance and fall flat on your face, it won't be graceful...and you'll be looking for another job."

This is a highly competitive industry where "you're only as good as your last hit film." The four years you have spent studying your art must be placed on the back-burner for now, and your focus must be turned to the "business" of the film industry.

The first thing you need to ask yourself is "Who am I?" or "What am I?" What are you, based on your background and experience to date? What can you do? What can't you do? And finally, what do you want to do?

When I interview students coming right out of college, the first question I ask them is, "If this were a perfect world, and you could do anything you wanted to do to make a living, what would that be, where does your passion lie, where would your heart lead you?" You'd be surprised how many students can't answer that question. They have only the vaguest idea what they want to do, even though they spent the last four years working towards a degree in English, or a degree in Radio & Television Communications, or a degree in Drama. So, let's try and answer these questions.

WHO AM I & WHAT AM I?

If your resume indicates that your theater experience is primarily as a Technical Director, then it is natural for you to think that's who you are. If it shows Lighting Design as your major focus, then it is natural for you to think that you are a Lighting Designer. If it indicates that you've directed short films, then you naturally believe that you're a Director. If it shows you performed in mostly serious roles in stage plays, then it is natural for you to think that you're an actor who is typecast in serious roles. But, when you begin your career in the film industry, you need to go beyond that. " Who am I?" now has to mean "Where do I fit in the marketplace?"

WHAT CAN I DO, WHAT CAN'T I DO?

You must be brutally honest with yourself to know what you can and cannot do. Your experience may have taught you how to light a stage, but that doesn't mean you can light a film set or television set, for that matter. You may know how to perform Mercutio in "Romeo & Juliet" on the stage, but that doesn't mean you know how to work in front of a camera. Accept the fact that right now, at the beginning of your career, you're limited by your lack of experience. However, a lack of experience is not a detriment. More opportunities will come in due time.

WHAT DO I WANT TO DO?

Let us say that you want to be an actor. Does that mean you want to be a leading man/woman, a character actor/actress, a comedian, etc.? If you want to work in one capacity or another behind the camera, what capacity is that? For example, do you want to be a cameraman, director, producer, art director, etc. Do you even know what role everyone plays behind the camera?

This part of the book is designed to help you answer these and many more questions while helping better prepare you for finding your first employment opportunity. Not everyone will be seeking the same career, so the book has been split into sections for each area of interest, corresponding to the sequence of events which occur in the making of a film:

The Writer

The Producer

The Director

The Actor

Film Technicians

Studio Executives

After you read the section which relates to your own career interest, you should consider reading all of the other sections: it is, for example, of immense value to an aspiring actor's future success if he understands a director's mentality. Likewise, a director must be able to interpret the writer's intentions in his screenplay as clearly as if he wrote it himself.

If you do as I suggest, you'll find that, of necessity, certain subjects are repeated. However, they have been adjusted to fit the needs of the particular career discipline and will go a long way to your understanding of the "reel" business.

THE WRITER

NOTHING HAPPENS WITHOUT A SCRIPT

"Nobody knows anything."

> - screenwriter William Goldman on
> Hollywood from his book *Adventures
> In the Screen Trade*

In the film industry, the Writer is the person who creates the text from which the visual image is generated. It can be a theatrical motion picture screenplay, a direct-to-home-video motion picture screenplay, a cable or pay-per view motion picture screenplay, a motion picture for television teleplay, a television episodic script, a television sitcom script, a television commercial script, a television musical, comedy, or variety special script, a reality-based drama script, or even an industrial film script.

Nothing in motion pictures or television happens without a script. But being the original creator of one of these scripts and having it purchased by a producer, studio or television network is as difficult as climbing Mt. Everest: it can be done, but only the talented, flexible and persistent succeed.

How tough is it really to sell a screenplay? Sam Kitt, Head of Development for Spike Lee's production company, once said: "It takes 5 yeses to get a screenplay produced. And for every one yes, you will almost certainly have received 100 no's." In other words, selling a screenplay is one of the toughest sales jobs in the world. A writer must not only be talented, he must be quick at re-writing, be open and responsive to criticism and change, and a master of the "Art of the Pitch".

Producer Chip Diggins told me, "I read close to 500 scripts a year, get the opportunity to maybe develop 10 of them, and if I'm lucky, I'll get a greenlight to produce maybe two of them." That's how tough it is to sell a screenplay (incidentally, the term "greenlighting" is the expression used when a studio gives the go-ahead to produce the screenplay as a motion picture).

Currently, there are over 10,000 members of the Writer's Guild Of America (WGA). Each of these members write about three screenplays a year, and don't forget the non-union writers who also create roughly 20-25,000 screenplays each year. Combine the two groups and the marketplace is flooded with some 50,000 screenplays, from which roughly 300-400 films are produced annually. A longshot at the racetrack has better odds!

It is critically important to any beginning writer to understand, appreciate, and accept one aspect of writing for films: the task of converting a story into a screenplay and a screenplay into a film is rarely the product of just the writer. The director and even the producer are brothers to the writer. Thus, the process of taking an idea and turning it into a screenplay, although usually the responsibility of the writer, becomes a truly collaborative process between the writer, director and producer. Each may approach the process in a slightly different way: all three may actually write; the writer may write while the director gives notes on changes and the producer gives the final notes; the director or producer may develop an idea on their own and work with a writer to flesh out the story and screenplay, etc. Any way that it happens, the basics are essentially the same.

I will explain the process of developing screenplays as it is usually learned by the writer. But bear in mind that, in the end, it would serve any beginning writer well to read the sections in this book about directors and producers.

THREE PRIMARY TOOLS OF THE TRADE

Just as a plumber needs his monkey wrench, a fireman needs his axe, and a carpenter needs his hammer, a writer needs his tools. You may think this means a typewriter, some paper, and even a bottle or two of White-Out™. While these can certainly be useful, let us begin instead with the three most important items a writer must have before he even begins to type.

An Idea

To start your screenwriting career, the first thing you need to have is an idea. Back in the days when Studio Bosses like Louis B. Mayer and Jack L. Warner were running the film business, an individual could come up with an idea for a story, tell it to a studio boss, and if the boss liked it, sell it to the studio. He would then be given an opportunity to write the screenplay for which he was also paid. Those days are long gone. Studios rarely buy ideas or treatments anymore (treatments are essentially a brief synopsis of the story, usually no longer than 15 pages). The studios would much rather have the finished product, the screenplay. While a beginning writer can still pitch a story to a studio Creative Executive or independent producer, at the end of the day, all that really matters is whether or not the screenplay is any good. Nevertheless, the whole process starts with an idea.

So what is an idea? An idea is a concept, a thought, or a notion. It is a simple, one-sentence plan for a story. It can be as simple as "Boy Meets Girl" or "Boy Meets Girl, Boy Loses Girl, Boy Gets Girl Back." That sounds trivial, I know, but successful motion pictures have been sold on as little as that. I have heard that actor/comedian Paul Reiser sold the concept of the hit television show "MAD ABOUT YOU" with this simple concept: "THIRTYSOMETHING, only funny!"

Ideas can be found anywhere: from a newspaper article, from a conversation overheard in a restaurant, from an article read on the Internet, even from watching two kids playing on a swing in the park. Ideas are all around you. Keep your eyes and ears open and you'll find them. In fact, to keep your creative juices flowing, make it a point to come up with five new story ideas every day. Write them down and collect them in a card file. After you've collected 50 or so ideas, take a moment to read them aloud to yourself and see which idea is the first idea that jumps out at you as interesting. That's the idea you should begin developing into a story.

As a famous example, in a magazine article it was indicated that syndicated columnist Art Buchwald has been coming up with ideas for over 15 years and pitching them to the studios. Most of these ideas had been written in "treatment" form, but never developed as screenplays. Buchwald got lucky with one of them and sold his treatment to Paramount Pictures for which he was to be paid $65,000 if a film was made based on his story.

The operative word in this example is **"if"**: **"if"** a film was made from Buchwald's story. The story may be great, but if a screenplay cannot be developed from the story, then the story isn't worth the paper it's written on. Buchwald's sale of a treatment is one of very few such sales that have happened in the film industry in the last ten years: as I said, studios want to see completed screenplays.

Incidentally, a film entitled "Coming to America" was made based on Buchwald's treatment and was a tremendous success for Paramount Pictures. Buchwald subsequently sued Paramount for his share of the profits (see Chapter Eleven, "Creative Accounting", from the book *Dealmaking in the Film & Television Industry* by Mark Litwak). Buchwald's story is that exception to the rule. Nine and a half times out of ten, you won't be able to sell an idea; you'll need to sell the screenplay.

A Story

Once you have an idea that you think will "work," you need to set about developing a story or treatment. Since this is not a book about "how to" act, direct, write, etc., I will assume that you, the reader, know the basics of how to write a story. If you don't, stop reading now, run to a bookstore and pick up a copy of a "how to write screenplays" book such as *Screenplay: The Foundations of Screenwriting* by Syd Field, or *Making a Good Script Great* by Linda Seger.

Your story or treatment at this point need not be written in full sentences, but rather a set of note cards with either sentence fragments, one or two key words, or a brief description of the action that moves the story along.

The Art of Storytelling

Storytelling is an art form. It can be learned and mastered. It's easy to read a classic book like Bram Stoker's *Dracula* and immediately become enmeshed in the story. The book is filled with vivid adjectives and adverbs that paint an image so macabre and horrifying that you can't wait to read on to see what will happen next. For a film, a writer, doesn't have the luxury of relying on adjectives and adverbs - he must paint the images visually and carry the storyline through editorialized sequences of action, drama and suspense.

If you haven't yet written a screenplay that has been produced as a feature film, let alone a short film, a commercial, a play, or any presentational piece of entertainment, you'll need to begin developing your storytelling skills. You can start by purchasing a book of short stories. Read the first story over and over again until you fully understand the plot, intimately know the characters and what makes them tick, and are capable of dissecting the conflicts woven in the story. Once you're confident you have a full grasp of the story, invite a friend or two over for a cup of coffee and tell them about the short story you've just read. "Act it out" as passionately as you can as you try and involve your listeners in the story. Feel the emotion of every character as you describe their conflicts, fears, and joys, until you have the full attention of your listeners.

When you've finished telling your story, listen to the comments you receive from your audience. Did they like the story? Were they moved? Did they understand the plot or did they become confused by what they heard? If they don't offer, make sure to ask them their thoughts on the way you told the story: were there things you did during the storytelling that grabbed their attention and made them want to know more? If you stumbled over a section of the story, were you aware of it? Did the audience seem aware of it? Could it have been more smoothly presented? Take notes on what they say so you can polish the way you present the story the next time you tell it to someone. In fact, you can even consider audio or videotaping the telling of the story as well as the comments you receive. Then you can go back at your convenience and match your story points to the comments.

Mastering the art of storytelling is key. If you can tell a story, then you can write a screenplay and decipher where it works and doesn't work. And, as a writer, if you can't develop a strong screenplay and ultimately pitch it successfully to a studio creative executive, you'll be spending a lot of time at the Unemployment Office. What it means to "pitch" a screenplay will be discussed a little later in this section. First, let's concentrate on the screenplay itself.

Developing The Screenplay

Before you can begin developing the screenplay, you need to know the basics of what makes a good screenplay. This actually goes hand-in-hand with storytelling.

A good writer (as well as the director and producer) will spend time developing this skill by deciphering the elements of storytelling: Plot, Character, Conflict, Drama, Resolution, and so on. For example, an individual cannot build a car unless he knows the basics of what makes it run. He needs to dissect the engine, examine the pistons, determine the fuel source and understand how the fuel source is ignited to drive the parts of the engine into motion. Without this basic knowledge, he cannot build the vehicle. Later on, after he has studied the fundamentals of the engine, he can begin to tinker with his own ideas and build on the basics, occasionally creating a new way of looking at the engine, maybe even designing a more efficient and exciting machine.

The same holds true of the writer. He must study the screenplay in its most basic form, examine the elements of the story and become fully conversant in the many styles, techniques, and parts that together comprise the final product: a film. Plot points, conclusions, character growth, internal character conflicts, action beats, and other elements (the terminology varies depending upon which school you attended) are all key to developing a successful screenplay. Think of a few films which you feel told a wonderful story and analyze how the writer told it and why he made the choices he did. This will give you some strong insights into the art of telling a story.

If you are unsure of your abilities in storytelling, then before even attempting to write a screenplay, I encourage you to involve yourself in more study through either the American Film Institute's many seminars, or through the extension courses offered at UCLA. There are also a number of good books on the subject that are listed in the Appendix.

The Screenplay

Too often, beginning writers don't take the time to study the screenplay they've written, analyzing its elements to determine whether structurally it is ready for filming, whether the emotion of the story has been fully realized, and finally, whether the characters are interesting and ever-present. Once a budding writer feels confident with the components of a screenplay, and has written one, the writer should then ask himself these six important questions:

- What is the Concept of the Screenplay? What is the essence of the story. For example, at it's root, the Sean Connery/Richard Gere/Julia Ormond film, *FIRST KNIGHT*, is a dramatic love story about sacrifice and betrayal.

- Who's Story is It? Who is the film really about? If it isn't easy to determine which character carries the story, chances are the screenplay is too convoluted to sustain itself as a film.

- Can I Define the Lead Character's Growth? If you cannot answer this question, then chances are the lead character has no growth throughout the course of the film. He learns nothing, he has no emotional beginning, middle and end. Without growth, your characters, and thus your story, will be boring.

- Does Every Scene Move the Story Forward? If you were to remove a scene from the story, would the story still make sense? Would there be a gap causing the reader to become confused, or at a loss for emotional connection? If so, then the scene moves the story forward. If you can remove the scene and never even know it was there, then it shouldn't have been in the screenplay to begin with.

- <u>Do I Care about the People in the Story and What Happens to Them?</u> In Melissa Matheson's classic screenplay, *ET: THE EXTRATERRESTRIAL*, the audience is so caught up in the plight of ET and Elliot that they go through an emotional roller-coaster as Elliot tries to save the alien creature from certain destruction by the authorities. The writer has so structured the scenes and the characters that the audience cares deeply for the little creature and for the young boy who knows he's losing his best friend when the alien returns home. If your screenplay has you caring this much about its characters, then you're onto something. If you don't care about the characters, then you shouldn't make the movie.

- <u>Are the Characters in the Screenplay the Kind that Make "Star Actors" or "Star Directors" Jump?</u> As you're reading the screenplay, if you can envision certain film stars in some of the roles, and believe, based on the type of work they may have done in the past, that they may want this role, chances are a studio executive could envision the same actor in the same role - which means the movie has "studio appeal."

If after reading your screenplay you are capable of answering these questions satisfactorily, then you probably have a good basic screenplay on your hands. However, if some of these questions have been left unanswered, you will want to spend more time, maybe a lot more time, developing the screenplay.

FUNCTIONAL TOOLS OF THE TRADE

We've examined the three primary tools a good writer must have: an idea, a story and a screenplay. The idea and the story can be typed in a simple paragraph/novel fashion. However, a screenplay must be typed in proper format in order for a producer, director, studio executive, or investor to read it. As such, you'll need a few more tools to make this happen.

Some people still work in the 19th century by writing their screenplays on paper by hand. If that's the only way you can do it, so be it. However, I would encourage you to step up to the 21st century and use either a typewriter, word processor, or computer, preferably the latter. If you don't own one, buy one. Remember, writing is a business just like any other. To make yourself more marketable, you must invest in yourself by investing in the proper tools. A plumber wouldn't begin repairing a drain without a wrench, so why should a writer begin writing a screenplay without the proper tools? And with the relatively inexpensive cost of computers these days, there's no excuse for being unprepared.

Computer/Word Processor & Printer

Years ago, when I was still in college, most of my playwright classmates wrote their scripts on a typewriter, recognizing that they could put more words and thoughts on paper with a machine than they could by writing with pen and paper. I, too, tried using a typewriter, but made too many mistakes as I typed and found myself at the end of an evening having gone through two full reams of paper and at least three bottles of White Out™. So I graduated to a computer with a spelling checker.

Today, the serious writer works on a computer and delivers his work fresh from a printer. With the advent of personal computers the size of small notebooks and weighing 6 pounds or less, writing on a computer has become the industry standard. Ten years ago, buying a computer was a major investment, with the cost of top-of-the-line home systems equaling the price of a small car. Today, a beginning writer can invest in a good, used computer with a monochrome monitor for a minimal amount of money. Used IBM-compatible and Windows™-based systems can be found for as low as $200 or $300 while used Apple systems (Mac) usually start around $500, and prices are still dropping (Windows™ is a software program for IBM-compatible computers that creates an on-screen image similar to that of a Mac computer).

For a time, IBM-compatible & Windows™-based systems were the preferred choice of most writers as they provided the greater choice of software packages and easy-to-use screenwriting software. However, in recent years, Apple systems (Mac) have become quite popular for their simplicity and competitive screenwriting applications. The book you are reading was created entirely on a Mac. The screenplays I write and develop are all written on a Mac. This doesn't mean that an IBM-compatible computer should not be considered. I began my working knowledge of computers on an IBM-compatible computer and switched to a Mac not by choice, but because my employer switched over to Mac and I had no choice but to learn them or find another job. Either system is easy to use - the choice is up to you.

If you decide you cannot afford to purchase a new or used computer, take a look at a good, used word processor. In general, word processors cost less than personal computers and can provide you with an easy platform on which to write your screenplay. The down side of a word processor is that it only provides one application - word processing - whereas a computer can provide multiple applications supportive of screenwriting: calendars, film scheduling, film budgeting, and research databases, to name but a few. With the cost of computers only a few dollars more, word processors could soon disappear. Your best bet is to buy a computer, new or used when you can afford it.

You'll also need to purchase a printer. There are basically two types of printers on the market today: ink jet or laser printers. Whichever type you purchase, make sure that it has post-script software installed. The real questions you must consider are these:

- what type of printing quality do you want (letter quality vs. draft quality)?

- how quickly do you want to print pages (4 pages per minute vs. 1 page per minute, etc.)?

- do you require a printer with graphics capabilities?

The more requirements you place on your printer, the more expensive it will become. I prefer a laser printer because, to me, quality is the most important factor. I'm not worried that it may take an hour or so to print out all 120 pages of my screenplay, as long as it looks professionally prepared (the standard professional screenplay font is the `courier` font.) I invested in a laser printer which prints 5 pages per minute, that today would cost about $300. I could just as well have purchased an ink-jet printer. Its font type is very similar, it does a darn good job, and it costs half the price of a laser printer. It was simply a personal choice. Since you're just starting out, and your money situation may be tight, an ink-jet printer may be your best bet.

Invest in your career whenever you can! Don't feel you have to buy the Rolls-Royce of computers or printers, but at the same time, consider taking a step up from the bargain basement model. Shop around, ask questions, find the best deal, but don't start writing until you have invested in a system.

Computer Screenplay Software

It is difficult enough to write a screenplay without having to create your own stylesheet with which to format the text (a stylesheet is a page format which the computer or the writer will create that establishes the overall look of the finished page, e.g., margins, borders, bold-face type, etc.). Software is currently available which will format your text as you write, allowing you to focus on developing the creative aspects of your screenplay rather than worry about the margins and spacing.

The two most widely used screenplay writing software programs are Final Draft™ and Screenwriter™. Final Draft™ is widely regarded by writers, directors and producers as "the only choice" when it comes to writing your screenplay on computer. However, Screenwriter™ has begun to challenge it. With Final Draft™, your script is automatically formatted as you type. The format settings can be easily adjusted for feature screenplay, sitcom, episodic, movie-of-the-week, and stage play scripts. Some of the other highlights of Final Draft™ are:

- Master Character Lists - enter just enough letters to match the desired character's name and the software fills in the rest auto-matically.

- Automatic Pagination - includes MORE's, CONTINUED's, revision marks, A and B page numbering and more.

- Script Notes - floating note windows which can hold ideas, suggestions, reminders, or script fragments without affecting the script itself.

- Import/Export filters - a mechanism which allows you to transfer information from other sources in and out of your computer so you can easily work on scripts even though they may have been written on another computer or word processor

- Shortcuts - automatically switch from character name (all caps, centered) to dialog format by pressing the carriage return; no other scriptwriting program has it.

- Pre-Set Industry Standard Margins & Styles

• <u>Built-in Spell Checker and Thesaurus</u>

Final Draft™ costs approximately $300 and is currently available for both Mac & Windows™-based computer systems. You can also purchase Final Draft™ through MacMall Mail Order Catalogue (800-222-2808) and MacWarehouse Mail Order Catalogue (800-255-6227). Both companies sell the software for approximately $250.

Final Draft™ also has a companion software program available called Three By Five™. Three By Five™ offers three dimensional graphic outlining for the Mac. It incorporates advanced word processing and information management tools in a familiar format: index cards on a bulletin board. Three By Five™ can find, replace, categorize and arrange your information in a 3-D branching structure or completely at random. Information created and stored in Three By Five™ can even be transferred or imported into Final Draft™ giving you a starting point from which to begin writing your screenplay. Three By Five™ costs $69 and is also available for both Mac and Windows™-based computer systems.

Screenwriter™ is also a script-writing software program, functioning much in the same way as Final Draft™. However, Screenwriter™ communicates directly with Movie Magic™ Film Scheduling, allowing scene numbers, scene headings, page counts, and characters from your script to be imported directly into the film scheduling software. This task creates a substantial time saver for production managers. In addition, while Final Draft™ has a companion index card system sold separately, Screenwriter™ has its index card system built in already, at no extra charge.Screenwriter™ costs $299 and is currently available for both Mac and IBM-compatible computer systems.

Resource Books

Sounds obvious, but a dictionary is an extremely valuable tool. If you're working on a word processor or typewriter which doesn't provide a mechanism for checking your spelling, you'll need a dictionary to make sure your work is correct. There's nothing worse than reading a script that is filled with misspelled words. You don't need a giant-sized hard cover version. A simple pocket dictionary, such as the Merriam-Webster Pocket Dictionary™, will do.

As a writer, you need a command of the English language. A thesaurus will help fill in those areas of the language you can't remember from high school or college because you fell asleep in class. And it can help turn a simple image into a scene of explosive expression. When I first began writing, if I couldn't find just the right words for an image, I scratched on the paper the general idea of what I wanted to say. Then, later on, I came back to the section with my thesaurus and, quite literally, recreated the entire image, transforming the language from a simple, straightforward thought to an image of vast details, intricacies, and emotions.

Another valuable tool is the *Dictionary of Confusable Words*. While you may think your mastery of English is profound, tell me this: what is the difference between club soda and seltzer? Don't know? Well this book does. And it will keep you from discombobulating even the most sophisticated malapropisms. Oh......by the way..........club soda is fizzy water that may contain salt or other sodium compounds while seltzer is the same thing....but without the salt.

PROTECTING YOUR WORK FROM THEFT

When you finally have your screenplay completed and you're confident enough in it to begin having it read by others, **don't** immediately send your screenplay out to agents, producers and studio executives. Before you let anyone look at what you've created, you **must** protect your work so no one else can steal it. Here are three things you can do:

- Register your work with the WGAw - the WGAw will keep a written registration of your work in it's files for 5 years, renewable in five year increments. They accept written motion picture or television concepts, treatments, and scripts. They do not accept manuscripts or stage plays (try the Dramatist's Guild for stage plays). You cannot register by mail, you must appear at the WGAw's registration window in person to register. Bring with you an unbound copy of your work with a check made out to the WGAw for $20. In return, you will receive a receipt from the WGAw indicating the date of registration and the registration number assigned to the work. For more information about registering with the WGAw, call their pre-recorded hot-line at (310) 205-2500.

- Mailing a Copy to Yourself - enclose a copy of your work in a sealed envelope and mail it certified mail with a return receipt to yourself through the U.S. Postal Service. When you receive the work in the mail, *don't open it*. Lock it away in safe keeping where you know you'll always find it should you ever need it for legal reasons. If you want to go one step further, send the same kind of package certified mail with a return receipt to a neutral third-party who will swear, in a court of law if the need ever arises, that he received the package on a certain date and has kept it locked away ever since. Might not be a bad idea to mail both packages.

• <u>Copyright and Register Your Work</u> - contrary to popular belief, one does not need to hire a copyright attorney to copyright one's work. Anyone can copyright their work. However, not every piece of work is copyrightable. To copyright your work, you must meet four requirements. It must be:

  • original

  • an expression of an author

  • of a non-utilitarian nature (for example, an ordinary lighting fixture cannot be copyrighted because it is considered utilitarian. However, a statue is an aesthetic work that can be copyrighted.)

  • in a fixed, tangible medium of expression

For detailed definitions of these four requirements, contact the Library of Congress in Washington, D.C. or read the chapter on copyrights from the book *Dealmaking in the Film & Television Industry* by Mark Litwak.

If your work meets these four requirements, you may then copyright your work. A proper copyright includes the following information displayed on your work in a conspicuous location (on the back or inside of the cover page for example):

- the word "copyright"; the abbreviation for the word "copyright"; or the © symbol

- the name of the copyright owner (your full name is not required)

- the date of the first publication

You can also add the phrase "All Rights Reserved" which may provide protection if you encounter problems in foreign countries. Once you've done this, by law as stated in the 1988 Amendments to the 1976 Copyright Act, your work has been copyrighted. The length of duration for your copyright will last your lifetime plus 50 years, at which time the work will enter the public domain.

If you plan to publish your work, it's a good idea to register the property with the Library of Congress (LOC). The advantages to having your work registered with the LOC are plentiful (from the book *Dealmaking in the Film & Television Industry* by Mark Litwak):

- it establishes a public record of your copyright claim

- it secures you the right to file for any copyright infringements on works created in the USA

- it establishes prima facie validity of the copyright

- it opens up a broader range of remedies in an in-fringement suit allowing statutory damages and at-torney's fees

- registration gives the world notice of the copyright claim, even to those who may be unaware of the reg-istration

To register your copyright, send in the same envelope a completed application form, a non-refundable fee, and a copy of your work to the Library of Congress. The form and informa-tion on the fee can be obtained by calling the LOC at (202) 707-9100 or writing to them at Library of Congress, Washington, D.C., 20559. You are not required to publish your work, ever, but if you do publish it, you are required by law to send two copies of your work to the LOC within three months of publica-tion or be subject to fines.

CONSTRUCTIVE CRITICISM

Now that the screenplay is ready to be shown to people, first allow people whose opinion you trust to read it and be your critic. Preferably, give it to those who know and understand proper screenplay structure (three acts: set-up, confrontation, and resolution), character development (interior and exterior life, point of view, attitude, context, content, etc.), sequences, plot points, etc. Encourage them to write notes in the script as they read indicating questions and/or comments they may have.

It is probably not smart to have a family member read your work at this stage. Comments coming from a parent, brother or sister, or spouse may hurt your feelings and cause you to get defensive. Let them read it later, after someone skilled in reading scripts has offered constructive criticism and you've agreed upon changes.

After they've read it, take them to dinner and ask them for their honest opinions. Encourage them to go through the screenplay page by page giving you feedback about what works, what doesn't work, and anything they didn't understand. Take detailed notes about everything they say, regardless of whether or not you agree. Don't let your ego get in the way by confronting their criticism with anger, resentment or frustration. Remember, *you* asked for their opinion, the least you can do is listen to it and accept it. When you get home that night, put away your screenplay and notes for the night and go watch television or read a book. Do whatever you have to do, but don't work on or even think about the screenplay. You'll only find yourself getting all worked up about what your critic has said.

The next day, or even two days later, with your mind clear, go back through your notes and familiarize yourself with what your critic said. Then decide, without your ego getting in the way, if the comment, suggestion or criticism is valid and needs to be addressed in the screenplay. If it does, make a note to attack that particular problem in the script. If you don't believe it's valid, disregard it. But make certain your reasons are not ego driven and are because the comments will not help the script.

It's a tough thing to do, but one must be as humble as possible about criticism. Don't take it personally. The criticism is being offered because, to the reader, the text may not have made sense (although to you it may). To the reader, something may not be plausible, while to you, it couldn't possibly be anything but plausible. The reader is offering these thoughts because they want you to succeed, they want your screenplay to be the best it can be - that's why it's called "constructive" criticism.

PITCHING YOUR SCREENPLAY

With a finished screenplay, you can now begin the next important part of screenwriting - selling your screenplay. Everyone sells. Writers, directors, producers, even actors all must learn how to sell. Writers, directors and producers are generally selling the same thing - their product, which is the screenplay (actors, on the other hand, are selling another product: themselves). Everyone you talk to at any given moment should be considered a potential investor. As in any other industry, in order to get your product made, you must sell the buyers on the idea, convince them that your concept is the greatest. Selling, in the film industry, is done through a mechanism called "The Pitch."

Robert Kosberg, a television and film producer and author of the book *How To Sell Your Idea to Hollywood* says that pitching "is like telling bedtime stories to adults - enthusiastic, passionate and even more passionate."

The term pitching comes from baseball. The pitcher on a ball team has a selection of pitches he can choose from: a slider, a curve ball, a knuckle ball, a fast ball and so on. He selects his pitch, winds it up, and delivers it to the batter who "reads" the incoming ball to see if it is a pitch he likes. If he doesn't like what he reads, he lets the ball "pass" without hitting it. If he does like what he reads, he takes the pitch, hitting the ball into the field, hoping that it'll be a home run.

Baseball pitching correlates to screenplay pitching in the following manner. For this example we'll say that a writer is pitching his screenplay:

- the writer has a number of different screenplays to choose from: there's a thriller, a teenage comedy, a romantic comedy, an action film, and so on.

- with great excitement and enthusiasm, the writer selects his pitch and delivers a condensed version of the story to the Creative Executive, or CE (the person at a studio who must be convinced that the story can be made into a successful film).

- the CE listens to the story to see if it is a pitch he likes.

- if the CE doesn't like what he hears, he "passes" on the story without committing to it .

- however, if the CE likes what he hears, he agrees to read the screenplay, hoping that it'll be a box office smash.

The pitch is the writer's opportunity to sell the CE on the fact that his screenplay is the greatest screenplay ever written, has all the makings of a major hit, and is a project that the CE should definitely read.

There is a true art-form to pitching, one that can be learned and one that is only mastered through practice. Still, even the most practiced pitch does not always result in a sale. Be prepared for rejection - in fact, go into your pitch expecting not to sell it. Rather set your expectations on building a relationship with a new contact. That way, if the CE or producer suddenly shows an interest in your idea, it's a pleasant surprise, not a downer when he says "pass." More often than not, you'll pitch your screenplay and the CE or producer will say, "Thanks, but that one doesn't do anything for me. Do you have anything else?" If the question is asked, be prepared to answer. Although you may be coming in to pitch a completed screenplay, you probably have other story ideas that you have begun developing but for which you haven't commenced writing the screenplay. Know those ideas inside and out so you can offer up those ideas as well. You never know if one of those ideas will spark the interest of your listener.

No two projects are ever pitched in the same way because each project has its own unique personality. However, all pitches can be approached with the same basic skills and rules.

The Process

The process of pitching is relatively simple. Start with small talk: try and put yourself and your listener at ease. If the CE or producer ask you to get right to it, jump in. State the title, stress the central concept in one or two sentences, then get into the story. Tell the beginning, middle and end touching on the major plot points. If asked, go into further detail on the story and characters, letting them come alive with your descriptions (remember storytelling?). At the end of the pitch, ask your listener if he has any questions. If he has none, ask if he would care to hear any other ideas. If he asks to see the screenplay, have a copy with you that you can leave with him. Finally, thank him for his time and leave.

Time

A pitch for one screenplay or idea should never last longer than 10 minutes. It's important to know when you're about to overstay your welcome. Get in and get out so you'll be invited back to pitch again on another day. If asked for additional ideas or projects you're working on, give each concept 30 to 60 seconds, and pitch as many genres as possible. Always go in with more than one idea - in case your main story pitch doesn't sell, you'll have other stories you can pitch.

Speaking of time, it is probably a good idea to schedule your pitch meeting before 12:30PM. Why? Because by 12:30PM, most executives are hungry and are thinking about their upcoming lunch meeting, where they will be dining and with whom they will be dining. All this means is that they won't be focused or concentrated on your pitch and you'll lose out on a good opportunity. In addition, don't arrange to pitch too soon after lunch. You know how it is after you've had a good lunch - you just want to loosen the belt a notch or two, kick your feet up on the desk and take a nap. Once again, the executive's attention is not focused on the pitch. The ideal time for pitching is mid-morning or late afternoon.

Do Your Homework

Work on your pitch over and over again until you've refined it to a lean, exciting salespitch. Start with your story elements and condense them to their simplest form. Highlight only the juiciest plot points and cut out all extraneous details. Concentrate at all times on brevity and enthusiasm. If the story is a complicated one, you may want to set it up by giving some background first and then start in on the story. If you need to use notes to help cue you to key information during the pitch, write down these thoughts on 3x5 index cards and glance at them during your pitch. ***Do not read directly from the cards.*** Maintain eye contact with your listener. Try not to use props, they can be very distracting.

Attitude

The key to pitching is passion. When your love for your idea is evident, it helps sell your idea. Tell your story as if it was already up on the screen. Be passionate, enthusiastic, and committed (again storytelling). Being boring and unprepared is the kiss of death. Be articulate, brief and enthusiastic. A slow-going pitch can be saved by an outpouring of committed enthusiasm. Make it a fun experience for both you and the person to whom you are pitching. Your first few times out, you're bound to be nervous. But if you go into your pitch acting ill at ease, you're going to make the CE or producer, who are already under enormous pressure, feel even worse. So practice your pitch at home with a friend or in front of a mirror until you feel as relaxed as possible. Don't take criticism personally.

Expectations

Assume going into the pitch that you will not succeed, that the CE or producer may get bored by your pitch or just not like it at all. Go into your pitch with the expectation of building a relationship with a new contact and being invited back again to pitch something else. Remember, it is much riskier for a CE to say yes to a pitch than to say no (if they say yes, they then have to sell the idea to the boss who may not like it and may think the CE doesn't have much taste!).

If your listener seems distracted by something (the phone keeps ringing, they seem pressured, they're in a bad mood, etc.) or their eyes seem catatonic or glazed over, stop the minute you notice it and either move onto something else or get out of the room. Without calling attention to the distraction, try to reschedule the meeting by suggesting that you have some other ideas you'd like to pitch next week. And if *you* are having a bad day, don't pitch. Try to reschedule the meeting.

On the other hand, if a studio exec responds to your pitch positively and wants to be part of the development process by building on your story, keep your ego in check and welcome the input. As Robert Kosberg says, "Building a collaborative rapport with your listener is one of the best things that can happen in the idea-selling process because it indicates that the executive has already made a personal investment in your idea."

If you can't get a sense from your listener just what he thinks of your story, try asking in an "upbeat" way, "How does the idea sound to you?" If the response is evasive, ask the listener what appears to be wrong with the story. You might get input that can be helpful in improving the script.

Life After Pitching

If, after you've practiced and practiced and practiced and you find that you are just not an effective pitcher, don't be discouraged. Many of the top screenwriters, directors and producers working today cannot pitch effectively. But their work is still purchased. Why? Because, ultimately, the sale depends on the quality of the idea and how good the screenplay really is.

WRITERS FOR HIRE

One of the positive sides of having a screenplay read, even if it is not purchased, is the contact you have made. Although the CE or producer may not have liked your screenplay, it may simply be that he didn't like the story. However, he may have still recognized your talent. Your screenplay may indicate to him that you have a flair for strong characters, or a knack for realistic and catchy dialogue. Maybe you create strong visual action sequences. If the CE or producer is impressed with your talent, he will make a mental note about how you could be used in the future for script repair work or "script doctoring."

Back in 1988, *Time* magazine published an article about writers in Hollywood and how many of them are making very comfortable livings as screenwriters without ever having one of their screenplays produced. These writers were working as "screenplay doctors," rewriting other people's screenplays for a fee, but without receiving any form of screen credit in the produced film. Script doctors are paid on a project-by-project basis, anywhere from $75,000-500,000 depending upon the size of the rewrite and their reputation as writers. And, as *Time* magazine indicated, they can work on three or four films a year, making mid-six figures, and the public is unaware of their work because they receive no on-screen credit. When you work as a script doctor, you become a "Writer For Hire." In simple terms, this means that you retain no rights to the work you have helped create and for which you have been paid.

If your ego is such that you don't need to see your name on a theater or television screen, then a career as a script doctor should be strongly considered. You can work a lot, express your inner creativity and have a very lucrative career.

Keep in mind that most "writers for hire" don't begin their careers by being paid a fee of six figures. In order to reach that level, you'll need a few years of experience and some minor success with your writing. More importantly, you'll first need to join the writer's union.

Getting Into the WGA

The union which represents writers for the motion picture and television industry is the Writers Guild of America. The Writers Guild has two branches; one which represents writers in the Eastern United States, abbreviated as WGAe, and one which represents writers in the Western United States, abbreviated as WGAw. For the purposes of this book, we'll focus on the branch located in Los Angeles, the WGAw.

To join the WGAw, as with any other union, you must meet a number of requirements. The WGAw list their requirements in the form of "credits." Credits can be obtained by performing writing services for a WGAw signatory company. The ype of project you are writing will dictate the number of credits you receive. To be eligible for membership in the WGAw, a writer must receive a total of 12 credits accumulated within the preceding two years. Those credits are awarded as follows:

2 units	for each week of employment on a week-to-week or contractual term basis
3 units	a story for a radio or television program less than 30 minutes shall be prorated in increments of 10 minutes or less
4 units	a story for a short subject theatrical film of any length or for a radio program or television program or breakdown for a non-prime time serial 30 minutes through 60 minutes
6 units	a teleplay or radio play less than 30 minutes shall be prorated in 5 minute increments; or television format for a new serial or series; or "Created By" credit given
8 credits	a story for a radio or television program or breakdown for a non-prime time serial more than 60 minutes and less than 90 minutes; or screenplay for a short subject theatrical film or for a radio play or teleplay 30 minutes through 60 minutes
12 units	"story for a radio or television program 90 minutes or longer or story for a feature length theatrical film; or breakdown for a non-prime time serial 90 minutes or longer; or a radio play or teleplay more than 60 minutes and less than 90 minutes"

24 units   screenplay for a feature length theatrical film; or
                a radio play or teleplay 90 minutes or longer; or
                bible for any television serial or prime-time mini-
                series of at least 4 hours; or long-term projection
                which is defined as a bible, for a specified term,
                on any existing, 5 times per week non-prime time
                serial

Upon the receipt of 24 credits or more, you are eligible to join the WGAw. All you need do then is complete an application which can be obtained from the WGAw office in West Hollywood and furnish a non-refundable initiation fee of $2,500.

Membership in the WGAw will insure that you are paid at least the minimum rates negotiated by the WGAw with the Association of Motion Picture and Television Producers, or AMPTP. The AMPTP represents producers and studios in the film and television industry and collectively negotiates union agreements for them.

The current WGAw rates are broken into two divisions, high budget and low budget. High budget is defined as a feature film with a budget of $2,500,000 or more. Low budget is defined as a feature film with a budget less than $2,500,000. The current WGAw minimum compensation is as follows:

HIGH BUDGET
        Story $21,244
        Original Treatment   31,865
        Treatment   21,244
        First Draft Screenplay   31,865
        Polish   10,620
        First Draft Screenplay or Rewrite   21,244
        Screenplay, excluding Treatment   47,791

Screenplay, including Treatment   69,112

LOW BUDGET

Story	$13,935
Original Treatment	19,243
Treatment	13,935
First Draft Screenplay	16,725
Polish	6,971
First Draft Screenplay or Rewrite	13,935
Screenplay, excluding Treatment	23,223
Screenplay, including Treatment	37,165

For more information about the WGAw, contact the Business Agent at the WGAw office. The address and phone numbers are listed in the Appendix.

THEATRICAL STAGE PRODUCTIONS

While pitching is one way of showcasing your work, there are other ways to get your name on people's lips and peak their interest in seeing your work. If you are truly a writer, not just a director or producer trying to develop your writing skills, one of those ways is by writing stage plays. The theater world of Los Angeles is vast. There are over 200 theaters in Los Angeles, ranging in size from 99-seat Equity-waiver houses (theaters where Equity allows its members to perform, but waives most of its union protections while doing so) to the 3200-seat Dorothy Chandler Pavilion. The abundance of theater spaces provides a wonderful opportunity for writers to showcase their work.

For a complete listing of theaters in Los Angeles, contact Dramalogue magazine and ask to purchase a copy of their legitimate theater guide. It is always available and is updated at the end of each calendar year. See the Appendix for their address.

While almost none of the Equity theaters (Mark Taper Forum, Pasadena Playhouse, etc.) will accept unsolicited material, most of the smaller theaters in town will read original plays by unrepresented writers. However, you have to stay on top of them to read it. A writer friend of mine has sent ten of his plays over time around town to the various theaters only to have months go by without any response from them at all. Only after his consistent prodding has he been able to obtain a response, many of which were negative. Nevertheless, his perseverance has paid off with four of the ten plays being given full productions (the other six he produced himself in rented theater spaces).

If a theater likes your work, chances are they'll mount a production of your play for a limited run, usually about six weeks. Some will offer a negotiated flat fee up front for the right to produce the work, while others may share a percentage of the net box office with the writer ("net" is generally defined as the profits remaining after all investments have been repaid and all operational expenses have been reimbursed). Still, some others don't financially compensate the writers at all - they feel the opportunity to showcase the writer's work is compensation enough.

A production of the writer's stage play is a wonderful opportunity for the writer to invite CE's, producers, agents and other interested parties to see the writer's work. Although they'll be seeing a stage play and not a screenplay, in the bigger realm of things, what they'll really be seeing, hopefully, is talent. You may have made a connection by pitching, but they chose not to read anything you've written. Here is an opportunity for them to see a fully fleshed-out idea, character development, story structure, humor, etc. A stage production can help take a simple "pitch relationship" to the next level.

If you're having a play produced, you need to get the word out. Send a postcard to your interested parties inviting them to watch the production. Wait one week after mailing the card before following it up with a phone call to personally invite the guests to a performance. An example of a postcard, similar to the ones used in Figures 3 and 4, is illustrated in Figure 5.

STUDENT FILMS

If stage plays aren't your thing, try a student film. Los Angeles is the home of three institutions with prestigious film training programs:

- American Film Institue (AFI)

- University of California at Los Angeles (UCLA)

- University of Southern California (USC)

The phone numbers for each of these schools can be found in the Appendix.

Dear Mr. Creative Executive,

My new play, "Making A Star" is about to open. "Making A Star" is a drama in two acts about two gamblers who meet in a hotel room for their weekly gambling game of Russian Roulette. On this occasion, they bet on whether their third invited guest will play the game with them, only during this game...something goes terribly wrong.

"Making A Star" opens at The Court Theater, 722 N. La Cienega Blvd. In Hollywood, on Friday September 13th and closes on Friday December 24th. Performances are on Thursday, Friday and Saturday evenings at 8:00pm.

Please call me at 818-555-1000 to make a reservation for what I am certain will be a thoroughly enjoyable evening.

Sincerely,

Joe Writer

Mr. Creative Executive
Bigtime Productions
100 Anywhere Street
Los Angeles, CA 90038

EXAMPLE OF AN ANNOUNCEMENT POSTCARD

FIGURE 5

As part of their film school curriculum, advanced students at these schools are required to make films. The schools generally provide a film camera (usually 16mm), a few lights, a reel-to-reel tape recorder, and a small amount of 16mm film raw stock. Any additional equipment or money needed for supplies is usually up to the student. With limited funds and equipment, most student films are 15 minutes or less in length, but occasionally a longer length film is made. And on occasion, the film is produced on 35mm film.

Having seen many of the films produced by these students in the last 8 years, I can safely say that Steven Spielberg has nothing to worry about. The general quality of the films is good (camera, production design, costume design, editing, etc.). The biggest problems appear in the story and therefore provide a beginning writer the opportunity to practice his skills while assisting a student filmmaker. By listing your name and phone number on a note on these schools' call boards, you may be able to hook up with the next Robert Rodriguez and, together, conceive what could become an excellent short film. You won't get paid for your screenplay or story idea, but your work will be exposed to many people, including currently working, successful, film professionals.

Short films like these often go on to success at film festivals. Some are even entered into competition in the Short Subject Category at the Academy Awards.

THE PRODUCER

"BUT *WHAT* DOES A PRODUCER DO?"

"Producing movies can often be a bloodstained affair. But, if you can figure it out, it will definitely keep your pool heated."

- from *A Pound Of Flesh* by Art Linson

The one person involved in filmmaking who is probably the least understood and appreciated is the Producer. Why? Because most people haven't a clue as to what a producer actually does. A large part of what a producer does for a film is "behind the scenes" or performed long before the cameras ever start rolling. And then, when the camera stops, the producer is still there, long after the crew is gone and the film is weeks into editing. The producer is the first person hired on the film when it is greenlit, and the last person off the film after it has been released into theaters.

The "Original" Producer

In order to better understand the function of producers in today's film industry, we need first to go back and look at the role of a producer in the early days of filmmaking, in the days of Louis B. Mayer, Harry Cohn and Sam Goldwyn, when the motion picture studio bosses were king. Producers were hired under long-term, exclusive contracts to specific studios, and were assigned to films by the studio boss. The producer's job in this era was "to do it all" - make the film, i.e., translate the screenplay into a motion picture. He was, in fact, the filmmaker. He "produced" the finished reels of film. Hence, the title "producer." It didn't matter if he liked or believed in the script, or liked or believed in his lead actor, he had to "produce" the film or the studio boss would throw him out on his behind.

In those days, a film had only one producer. He had to understand and master *both* the creative and production aspects of filmmaking. More often than not, each producer was allowed to hire an assistant, titled the production manager, to help with the nuts and bolts of the film, but the Studio Boss relied heavily on the producer to keep the actors in line, keep the Director on schedule and on budget, and maintain the *Studio Boss's* artistic vision of the script. Remember, each film had only one producer.

Over the years, the producers began to appreciate the contributions being made by the production managers. It was often the unique knowledge, experience and input they provided that was critical to a film being efficiently and cost-effectively produced. Indeed, even the Studio Bosses began to recognize this contribution, and began to give producing credit to these production managers.

But, the Academy of Motion Picture Arts and Sciences only gives the Academy Award for Best Picture to the individual(s) who is given on-screen credit as "Producer." As a result, the original Producers began offering alternatives to the typical producing credit. Today, films can have many sub-producers on the payroll. Robert Redford's film "Quiz Show" had ten such sub-producers credited in the screen credits. However, only one (occasionally two or three) person gets the coveted title of Producer.

Defining The Many "Sub-Producers "

Today, films have become more complex than ever before. As a result of this complexity, the role of the "producer" has become specialized and even categorized. However, when stripped down to the bone, there are basically only two types of producers: Creative Producers and Line Producers. In their most simplistic forms, a Creative Producer deals with the screenplay, the actors and the director, while the Line Producer deals with the physical aspects of the film such as the budget, schedule, equipment, locations, crew, etc.

A Creative Producer is the person who usually is given the on-screen credit of Producer. As such, from here on, I will refer to Creative Producer simply as Producer.

The Producer is an individual who has great creative vision, terrific creative instincts, knows a great script when he reads one, and has a vast network of relationships with writers, directors, actors, studio executives and agents. A Producer is charged with the supervision of all creative aspects of the film.

A Line Producer is usually subordinate to the Producer and picks up where the Producer leaves off. A Line Producer is a hands-on person, with organizational, managerial, financial and political skills, often referred to as the "nuts and bolts," which he uses to manage the production of the film on a day-to-day basis.

Crediting the Many Producers

In an industry where the prevailing philosophy is, "you're only as good as your last film," producing credit is second in importance only to the salary you command. There are many credits given to producers, so much so that it can often become confusing, if not ridiculous. However, there is some logic to the system.

The "Executive Producer" credit is often given to the person functioning as a line producer. Most line producers would rather not receive credit as "Line Producer," for in their opinion, it suggests that the individual's contribution was only organizational, managerial and financial, but does not reflect the creative input that they invariably do make. Most line producers feel that an "Executive Producer" credit suggests a greater overall involvement. This is further supported by the fact that the "Executive Producer" credit is often given to the agent or manager of the star of the film when it is called for in the star's contract.

Also, independent film companies such as Miramax, New Line, and Castle Rock, often credit the executive who heads up the film production division of their respective companies with Executive Producer credit as a recognition of their contribution towards the film being made. Executive Producer credit is also given to the producer who set up the film or who originally found the screenplay, but may no longer be actively involved in the production of the film (setting up a film can be defined simply as arranging for the financing of the film, or convincing a studio or independent production company to finance the film).

The "Co-Producer" credit is occasionally given to production managers when a separate line producer has been hired on the film and he has already secured the Executive Producer credit for himself. Since the production manager may be looking to move his career into the producing world, he will often take on the task of production manager provided that he receive some kind of producing credit. Hence, Co-Producer.

At this point you may ask why would a film employ both a line producer and a production manager, if, essentially, both individuals are doing the same thing, managing the nuts and bolts of the production? This question can be answered in a number of different ways, but the most logical explanation is this: it is probably fair to say that during principal photography, the majority of a line producer's day is spent on the set, overseeing the director and insuring that the work planned for the day is being completed and that it is of the highest artistic quality. Meanwhile, the majority of the production manager's day is spent in the production office managing the day-to-day paperwork of the production, such as approving time cards, call sheets and production reports, reviewing and approving daily and weekly cost reports, closing vendor and miscellaneous equipment deals, and so on,

As you can see, there is enough work for two people, and sometimes even enough for three. While a line producer *can* do the jobs of both producer and production manager, and on some lower-budgeted productions he does, it is often easier, and in the best interest of the production if the roles of line producer and production manager are filled by separate individuals.

Then there is the Associate Producer. This ambiguous title can be given to a host of individuals. Although many hard-working individuals deserve this small recognition, too often these worthy people must share this credit on-screen with someone who truly doesn't deserve it. In those instances, it is given primarily for ego gratification. Individuals known to have been given this credit include agents, managers, assistants, stunt coordinators, production supervisors, post-production supervisors, 1st assistant directors, production managers, and on and on.

THE MAKINGS OF
A GOOD PRODUCER

It has been said that anyone can be a producer, that it takes no talent. If that were true, then EVERYONE would be a producer because a successful producer can make a lot of money. But it isn't as easy as it sounds. There is no exact science to finding a producing job in the film business. Everyone gets his first break in his own unique way. Some never get their chance. But since there are so few opportunities out there, you'll increase the odds in your favor and be light-years ahead of the competition by being well prepared. How? By mastering the specific tools of the producer to which the competition does not pay attention.

In the section entitled THE WRITER, I emphasized that process of screenplay development is a collaborative effort between the writer, producer and director. I also reviewed the three primary tools of the trade: an idea, a story and a screenplay. Nothing can happen unless a writer, producer or director have a screenplay. So if you skipped reading the writer's section, go back *now* and read it thoroughly. Once you've done that, we can address the one tool that a Producer uses that the Writer and Director don't: Packaging.

PACKAGING

Sometimes pitching your story is not enough. You pitch and pitch and pitch, but no one seems to be listening. So how can you make them listen? What one thing can you, a producer, add to the mix that will spark the interest of most industry professionals? The answer is talent.

Talent, for the sake of this section, is defined as a star-director or star-actor. A colleague of mine recently told me about a screenplay that she and her husband wrote and sold to MGM with themselves attached to produce the film. As excited as they were, they were also extremely frustrated. While MGM owned the screenplay, they weren't doing anything with it. It was simply sitting on the shelf. This was probably because the story was a "tough sell" - it had limited audience appeal. My colleague shared with me that the story was basically a slant on the successful "I Love Lucy" television series. You remember, the first successful sitcom starring Lucille Ball and Desi Arnaz? Well, their screenplay updated the White/Hispanic relationship and viewed it in a comic way.

Although Hispanic films have been "tough sells" for a long time, they are steadily gaining an audience with the help of skillful performances by Latino & Hispanic actors Antonio Banderas, Andy Garcia, Edward James Olmos, Salma Hayek, and others. Yet they still represent only a small market share of the film-going audience in the U.S. Apparently, MGM was moved by the screenplay enough to buy it, but they were struggling with how to market the film to a larger audience in an effort to make the film financially successful.

My colleague and I put our heads together and realized that the best way to help the film along was to package it with the right talent. Packaging means to attach a name director and/ or name actor that would excite a studio or investor enough to put up the money to make a film. Knowing this was a Hispanic story, we realized the film would not be given multi-millions of dollars for production but rather a more modest budget of two to five million. This also meant that we could not afford to hire name talent at their normal rate. The talent would have to cut their rate down because they believed in the film.

After discussing the characters in the film, my colleague and I came to the conclusion that we should first try and attach a director whose talent, credits and passion for the project would excite and interest name actors to commit to doing the film. We thought as a first step in the process we should try to contact director Robert Young. Although we did not personally know Mr. Young, we knew that the films he had directed (such as THE BALLAD OF GREGORIO CORTEZ and ROOSTER) were finely crafted examples of small independent films made on limited budgets which presented the Hispanic viewpoint. And the films were profitable.

We also knew that many of the films that Mr. Young had directed featured actor Edward James Olmos. And there just happens to be a prime lead role in my colleague's film for Edward James Olmos. So, if we could convince Mr. Young to read the script and he liked it, he might be helpful in getting the script to Mr. Olmos to read.

If Mr. Young would agree to direct it, and Mr. Olmos agree to star in it, my colleague and her husband would agree to produce the film for five million dollars, and we would then have a much more interesting "package" which may entice MGM to finance the film and give it the greenlight. All we would need is a letter from both Mr. Young and Mr. Olmos stating their commitment to participating in the film should the producers be able to secure the appropriate financing.

The ideas contained within the package may be successful, or like some other packages, not bear fruit. However, it is a prime example about how a successful producer *thinks* about packaging.

You can follow the same steps to help get your first film produced. But you must be clever about it. What I mean is that not every director and/or actor attached to the project will get the film made. Obviously you want to go after the biggest names that you can to attach to your film. But if you have difficulty with getting big names, try another approach - determine what the market is for your film, who the audience is, and just how much revenue can be produced by that audience. Then approach actors and/or directors who have experience with that market and pitch your story to them. If they're interested in the story, ask them if they will agree to give you a letter of intent, which will commit them to the project should you arrange the financing. This kind of packaging can take a stalled screenplay and turn it into an active film.

You will not always be successful in getting big box-office stars to commit to your film. Most likely, you'll only get non-stars to commit. That's okay. What you need to keep in mind, then, when pitching this new package is that although these talented people have less-proven track records than Tom Cruise and Ron Howard, they are truly the stars of tomorrow.

How to Contact Talent

Now you're saying to yourself, "Okay, but how do I get to these actors and directors? I'm a nobody. I don't know any of these people." Well, in the previous example of packaging I gave you, neither did my colleagues nor I. It goes back to the *networking* section. These talented people are not going to come to you. You must go to them. And if you don't know them, you need to find someone that you know who does! Here are just a few ways that you can contact actors and directors:

- Talk to people. Tell everyone you meet that you are a creative producer interested in contacting John Doe Director or Jane Doe Actress about reading your screenplay. Someone out there is going to know someone who knows someone else who is best friends with the assistant of the Director or the cousin of the Actress. Be persistent, take notes on who you've spoken to so you can follow up later, and keep trying! You may even get a home address for the director or actress. If that's the case, write a nice concise letter to the talent enclosed with the screenplay. State that you think they are perfect for this film you are trying to get made. Ask them if they would be interested in joining you on the project should you arrange financing. If you have their phone number, don't call them first! Send your letter, allow 1-2 weeks for them to read it, and then call them as a follow-up. Be polite and courteous. Don't be rude or pushy or you'll lose any hope of getting them involved. If they express interest ask them if they would be willing to give you a letter of intent. This will be proof to the studio that you have the talent you say you have.

- Attend Seminars. Sign up for a few of the screenwriting seminars where you'll get a chance to meet and talk with other industry professionals. Use this opportunity to talk to them about your screenplay and tell them who you are trying to contact. If they like you and your story, chances are they may be willing to help you get to the person you want to contact.

- Purchase a DGA Directory. The Directors Guild of America (DGA) is the union which represents professional directors in the film and television industry. Like most unions, once a year they publish a directory of the members which lists addresses, phone numbers, representation contacts and film credits for every member of the union. You can purchase a copy of the directory from the DGA or you can buy it at most industry bookshops such as Samuel French for

$25. Once you have it, read through and familiarize yourself with the many directors in the union. Note their credits. If any credit suggests to you that the films they've made are the kind of films that you want to make, or are similar in style, theme or content to the film you're selling, contact the directors and pitch them your story. If they like the idea, they may be willing to work on it with you. But don't take a "no" personally. It may not be what the director had in mind to work on next. You can always contact him again with another story idea.

- Call SAG for Contact Information: The Screen Actors Guild (SAG) is the union which represents professional actors in the film and television industry. You can reach the SAG Agency Listing office in Los Angeles by calling (213) 954-1600 and asking for the Agency Listing Department. When you give the operator the name of the actor you are trying to contact, they will tell you who their agent and/or manager is. You can then use this information to call the agent or manager and pitch the story to them in the hope that they will like it enough to set up a meeting or phone call for you with the actor to discuss the project.

- Academy Listing: The Academy of Motion Picture Arts and Sciences (AMPAS) publishes annually a pictorial listing of actors and their headshots. By browsing through the book, you can find the actor you are looking for and obtain the phone number of his agent and/or manager. You can then contact the agent and/or manager as I have already explained.

Finding a Writer

Producers and directors are not expected to write screenplays. On the contrary, that is why they hire writers! You should know, however, that in the medium of television, most producers are also the show's writers. But in film, the producer and director have the luxury of not having to write the scripts themselves. All they must do is read them and determine if they work. But in order to do this, a director and producer must have a screenplay to read, and if they have no relationships with writers, then how do they get screenplays to read?

There is no right or wrong way to obtain screenplays, but here are a few suggestions as to how you can develop relationships with writers so that you may read their work before anyone else does:

- Talk to People. Tell everyone you meet that you are a producer or director looking for screenplays and inquire as to whether they are writers or know of any writers who might allow you to read their work. You'd be surprised how many people write screenplays or have friends who are working on screenplays.

- Advertise. There are a number of film industry trade papers in which a director or producer can place an advertisement seeking screenplays. *Dramalogue, Daily Variety, The Hollywood Reporter* are just a few of the many trade papers. But keep in mind that you want your notice to appear in trades that are read by writers. If you don't know which ones those are, try contacting the Samuel French Bookshops in both

Los Angeles and New York to ask for their help with the names and addresses of trades which allow advertisements for the solicitation of screenplays.

- <u>Attend Seminars.</u> Sign up for a few of the screenwriting seminars where you'll get a chance to meet and talk with beginning writers. Take an active interest in them and ask to read their work. Offer your criticism only if they ask for it. Who knows, maybe some of your comments will help them to better understand where their screenplay is not working and they may be so impressed that they will be willing to work on the script with you guiding it as the producer!

- <u>Purchase a Writers Directory.</u> The WGAw, like most unions, publishes a directory of the members once a year which lists addresses, phone numbers, representation contacts and screenplay credits on every member of the union. Much like the DGA directory, you can purchase a copy of the directory from the union or you can buy it at most industry bookshops such as Samuel French for $25. Then use the directory in the same fashion as you would the DGA directory as I explained earlier.

WHO IS OFFERED
THE JOB OF PRODUCER?

The skills we have discussed will make you better prepared than the rest of your competition for finding your first opportunity for employment as a creative producer. But it doesn't guarantee a job. Even the most skillful creative producers must work to get one of his projects produced.

The key to finding work as a creative producer is in convincing someone in the industry that you know what you're doing. While that may sound trivial and simplistic, it is truly the key to finding that first job. Generally, a creative producer will be offered the opportunity to produce a film because of one of the following reasons:

- he wrote the screenplay and will not allow it to be produced unless he is hired as its producer

- he worked with the screenwriter in developing the screenplay and has an oral or written agreement with the screenwriter that he will produce the screenplay

- he has pitched the screenplay to the investor or studio executive who liked the pitch, read the script, and has agreed to finance the film

- he has produced at least one film previously that the investor or studio creative executive has seen and liked

- he has produced at least one film before that the investor or studio creative executive has seen and liked, AND that film made money

- the producer has a development deal with a studio and the studio offered him this film as part of his development deal

- the studio owes the producer a favor

If none of these applies in your case, then you have a tough task ahead of you. Still, you can be given a creative producing assignment simply on the basis that someone believes you know what you're talking about.

I have seen many a first-time creative producer be given a chance to produce a film when in fact they know nothing about the craft. They simply did a hell of a selling job. They impressed someone into believing that they understood the screenplay and that it would be a big success at the box office, and that they could deliver the film for a price. Why not go beyond this facade and prepare yourself as we've discussed? You'll find that more opportunities will be available if you truly know your craft.

THE LINE PRODUCER

Once the screenplay is set up and the financing is in place, then the role of the Line Producer begins. If the Producer can be likened to a Chief Executive Officer, then a Line Producer can be likened to the Chief Operating Officer of a company. He is responsible for the day-to-day operation of the film production, beginning with pre-production through the completion of principal photography.

The primary difference between a Producer and a Line Producer is this: Producers control their own destiny by "owning" property and selling it with themselves attached as producer; Line Producers are talent for hire, often hired by the Producer. As I said earlier in this chapter, the role of the Line Producer was created a number of years ago when studios began to realize that without the knowledge, experience and input of production managers, films would not be produced as efficiently and cost-effectively as they would be without their participation. Recognizing this contribution, studios began to offer production managers producing credit. Some people say that for the most part, a line producer is a production manager with a producing credit and a bigger paycheck, although there are just as many who would argue this fact. But a successful line producer, and one in demand, is much more than that.

A good line producer is knowledgeable about all aspects of film production. Not only should he be able to develop a film schedule and budget, and manage the film to that schedule and budget, a good line producer must be conversant in the overwhelming volume of union regulations. He must be familiar with and maintain a file of top-quality crew personnel who not only deliver the goods artistically, but financially as well. He must be a diplomat, a cheerleader, a cautious and objective support arm, and a strong communicator. He needs to be able to anticipate problems long before they ever occur and know just what to do if and when they do occur. And all along, he must walk the fence, maintaining the vision of the director while controlling the budget for the investor. A good rule of thumb for a line producer to follow is this: the best decisions are those made on the basis of what's best for the film, not what's best for the egos of the Producer, Director, or Star - although, sadly, this rule can often be broken for policy or political reasons. However, by maintaining the "what's best for the film" philosophy, a line producer will always be serving both the director and the investor.

Much like the Boy Scout who is taught to always "be prepared," a line producer must approach his film with the knowledge and confidence that he has done his homework. Too many times in Hollywood does one hear of a first-time line producer who has been given an opportunity to produce a film, and on day one of pre-production, he arrives in the production office without a clue about what to do first. Subsequently, the process of shooting the film becomes laborious and troublesome. Tensions mount, rumors abound, and the film comes in over budget and over schedule. Finally, the film is released and bombs, and the fledgling line producer's career is over. Why does this happen? Because too many young line producers think that the essence of producing a film is simply moving actors around in front of a camera. What they don't realize, until it's too late, is that there is a lot more to producing a motion picture than meets the eye.

Schooling for the Line Producer

As I've already illustrated, most line producers are or have been production managers. Most have been schooled in their jobs by having worked their way up the ranks from production assistant to assistant director, to production manager, regardless of whether or not they are in the union. It doesn't mean this is the only way to arrive at such a career. A number of the successful line producers working today never worked as production managers - and yet they bring to the job years of experience in management type positions (location managers, production supervisors, facility managers, etc.). However, the best training ground for a future production manager is by working within the structure established in the Directors Guild of America, or DGA.

Producers are not obligated to join the DGA. However, if you plan to work as a production manager on a union film, then you'll have to be a member of the DGA. As pointed out in the section entitled THE BASICS, the DGA represents Directors, Unit Production Managers (UPM, also called production managers), Assistant Unit Production Managers (AUPM), 1st Assistant Directors (1st AD), 2nd Assistant Directors (2nd AD), 2nd 2nd Assistant Directors (2nd 2nd AD), and DGA Trainees.

At the start of your career, you'll probably have an opportunity to produce or be the UPM of a few low budget productions long before you ever have an opportunity to work on a DGA supported project. So think twice before joining the union right away. It may not make sense early in your career to join as it may limit your employment opportunities (Golden Globe Best Director nominee Ang Lee, director of 1996's SENSE AND SENSIBILITY has had a long and prosperous career as a director without being a member of the DGA. Only now that one of his films has achieved such acclaim has he joined the DGA).

Roughly 85% of the productions in Los Angeles are staffed by DGA personnel. In general, the really low budget productions (films with production budgets of $1,000,000 or less) are staffed with non-DGA labor. All of the major studios are signatory to the DGA and as such are required to use DGA labor, regardless of budget size. If you are interested in becoming a member of the DGA, it's not that easy. Basically, there are two ways to get into the DGA: by applying to the DGA Contract

Administration Office and meeting the prerequisites, or through the Assistant Director's Training Program. For more details, read the section on Directors which explains how to join the DGA.

PRE-PRODUCTION:
COLLABORATING WITH THE DIRECTOR

Let's assume now that you have mastered the process of finding and developing a screenplay. The next step in making you better prepared than the rest of the would-be line producers is in understanding pre-production: the process of preparing a screenplay for filming. It is at this point that the line producer begins to collaborate closely with the director. Many of the key decisions made during this period are often made by the director and line producer together. *Although this falls under the PRODUCER section, if you wish to direct films, it is important that you read this section carefully as well.*

The Pre-Production Period

During this period, both the line producer and director must be organized, efficient, decisive, and able to manage a multiple personality production. Both must use this time wisely or fall victim to tension, stress, anger, frustration, and poor performances which are generated when the leader of the ship arrives on the set not knowing where to sail his vessel.

Generally, the line producer and director have only 10 to 14 weeks in which to prepare themselves and their production team for the beginning of photography. This planning or "home work" is essential. The line producer must immediately assume a leadership role by supporting and guiding his director toward making the many decisions needed to move the film forward to photography. First, with input from the director and production manager, the line producer must create a pre-production schedule or "prep schedule" so that he and the rest of the crew will know in advance the deadlines for key decisions. An example of a generic prep schedule is illustrated in Figure 6.

With the prep schedule completed, the director and production manager work together to create a shooting schedule which will determine the order in which the scenes will be shot. Shooting schedules can be as short as 15 days and as long as 100 days or more, depending upon the complexity of the scripted action, locations, and budget restrictions. The shooting schedule also provides the Casting Director with the knowledge of the number of working days an actor will be required for a particular role in the film, influencing the decision of which actors can be sought for key roles. The line producer should review this schedule and share with the director and production manager any thoughts or concerns he has about the production team's ability to meet this schedule and stay on budget. A good line producer will be diplomatic, contributing his thoughts without impinging on the director's self-esteem. A sample of a condensed version of a shooting schedule, called a one-line schedule, is illustrated in Figure 7. A one-line schedule condenses the often large amount of information about the scene into one succinct line of information, making it more manageable and easier for anyone to review it.

WEEK 12

- Director meets possible Casting Directors, Production Designers (PD), Directors of Photography (DP), Costume Designers (CD), and Editors

WEEK 11

- Start Casting Director
- Start PD and Location Manager (Loc Mgr)

WEEK 10

- Open Production Office
- Start Unit Production Manager (UPM)

WEEK 9

- Director Begins Casting Auditions
- 1st Location Scout (Director, Producers, Loc Mgr, UPM, and PD)

WEEK 8

- Director Continues Casting Auditions
- Director Locks in DP
- Start CD

WEEK 7

- Director Continues Casting Auditions
- Start DP for 1 week of prep prior to permanent hiring
- 2nd Location Scout (Director, Producers, Loc Mgr, UPM, PD and DP)

WEEK 6

- Director Continues Casting Auditions
- Lock-in Major Locations
- Start 1st Assistant Director (1st AD)

WEEK 5

- Director Continues Casting Auditions
- Shoot Screen Tests (if necessary, you'll start the DP here)

WEEK 4

- Lock in Cast
- Lock in Final Script

WEEK 3

- Shoot Makeup/Hair/Wardrobe Test
- Start DP full time

WEEK 2

- Start Cast Rehearsals
- Final Location Scout (Director, Producers, Loc Mgr and All Key Crew)

WEEK 1

- Continue Cast Rehearsals
- Start Film Editor

A GENERIC PREP SCHEDULE - FIGURE 6

```
-----------------------------------------------------------------
                    "WHO THE HELL IS CHIP GLASS?"
-----------------------------------------------------------------
                    A Los Angeles-based Production
-----------------------------------------------------------------
                    SAG/Non-DGA/Non-IA/Non-Teamster
-----------------------------------------------------------------
              25-day shooting schedule, 6-day shooting weeks
-----------------------------------------------------------------
        Pre-Production: April 6, 1998 to May 29, 1998 (8 wks)
-----------------------------------------------------------------
```

18	EXT	WORLDVIEW CABLE - PARKING LOT	DAY	4 / 8	BJ gives report.
20	EXT	WORLDVIEW CABLE - PARKING LOT	DAY	1 / 8	BJ answers questions.
22	EXT	WORLDVIEW CABLE - PARKING LOT	DAY	3 4/8	COOKIE & BJ have words.
50	EXT	WORLDVIEW CABLE - PARKING LOT	DAY	1 4/8	BJ & COOKIE at lunch.
53	EXT	WORLDVIEW CABLE - PARKING LOT	DAY	3 / 8	Everyone discusses Dirk.
		--- END OF DAY 1 -- Mon, Jun 1, 1998 -- 6 pgs.			
36	INT	WORLDVIEW CABLE - STAGE	DAY	1 / 8	Sumo Talk-Show is over.
8PT	INT	WORLDVIEW CABLE - STAGE	DAY	1 3/8	HOWARD is doing his show (FOR PLAYBACK).
10	INT	WORLDVIEW CABLE - STAGE	DAY	1 / 8	HOWARD is doing his show.
44PT	INT	WORLDVIEW CABLE - STAGE	DAY	1 / 8	CHIP gets pushed (FOR PLAYBACK).
44PT	INT	WORLDVIEW CABLE - STAGE	DAY	1 / 8	CHIP gets salsa dumped on him (FOR
44PT	INT	WORLDVIEW CABLE - STAGE	DAY	2 / 8	CHIP & JULIA ROBERTS (FOR PLAYBACK).
44PT	INT	WORLDVIEW CABLE - STAGE	DAY	4 / 8	CHIP & ROY ROGERS and DALE EVANS (FOR
44PT	INT	WORLDVIEW CABLE - STAGE	DAY	1 / 8	CHIP & ZSA ZSA GABOR (FOR PLAYBACK).
27	INT	WORLDVIEW CABLE - MAKEUP RM	DAY	5 / 8	CHIP is in makeup.
37	INT	WORLDVIEW CABLE - MAKEUP RM	DAY	2 / 8	BJ watches COOKIE at work.
47	INT	WORLDVIEW CABLE - MAKEUP RM	Morning	6 / 8	BJ & COOKIE talk to STEPHANIE.
49	INT	WORLDVIEW CABLE - MAKEUP RM	Morning	1 2/8	GIRLS ask STEPHANIE about Basil.
		--- END OF DAY 2 -- Tue, Jun 2, 1998 -- 5 5/8 pgs.			
32	INT	WORLDVIEW CABLE - COOKIE'S OFFICE	Morning	5 / 8	BJ apologizes to COOKIE.
33	INT	WORLDVIEW CABLE - HALL OUTSIDE COOKIE'S	Morning	5 / 8	BJ asks COOKIE for help.
35	INT	WORLDVIEW CABLE - HALL OUTSIDE COOKIE'S	Morning	3 / 8	BJ sees the craziness of the station.
34	INT	WORLDVIEW CABLE - PLAYBACK CENTER	Morning	1	BJ tells COOKIE her plan.
46	INT	WORLDVIEW CABLE - HALLWAY	Morning	3 / 8	BJ & COOKIE agree to talk to Stephanie.
48	INT	WORLDVIEW CABLE - HALLWAY OUTSIDE STAGE	DAY	6 / 8	STEPHANIE discovers CHIP crying.
62	INT	WORLDVIEW CABLE - GREEN RM	Morning	1 5/8	COOKIE & BJ discuss Mitzi.
67	INT	WORLDVIEW CABLE - COOKIE'S OFFICE	DAY	1 3/8	COOKIE talks with PABLO;
69	INT	WORLDVIEW CABLE - COOKIE'S OFFICE	DAY	4 / 8	COOKIE continues talking with PABLO.
		--- END OF DAY 3 -- Wed, Jun 3, 1998 -- 7 2/8 pgs.			
39	INT	WORLDVIEW CABLE - COOKIE'S OFFICE	Evening	2 5/8	BJ & COOKIE consider the clues.
41	INT	WORLDVIEW CABLE - COOKIE'S OFFICE	Evening	7 / 8	BJ & COOKIE consider tapes.
40	INT	WORLDVIEW CABLE - COOKIE'S OFFICE	DAY	3 1/8	CHIP argues about time slot.
44PT	INT	WORLDVIEW CABLE - GREEN RM	NIGHT	4 / 8	COOKIE mugs for camera (FOR PLAYBACK).
		--- END OF DAY 4 -- Thu, Jun 4, 1998 -- 7 1/8 pgs.			
8PT	INT	WORLDVIEW CABLE - COOKIE'S OFFICE	DAY	1 7/8	We meet COOKIE and WYSTERIA.
9	INT	WORLDVIEW CABLE - HALL OUTSIDE COOKIE'S	DAY	1 1/8	BJ meets COOKIE.
13	INT	WORLDVIEW CABLE - HALL OUTSIDE COOKIE'S	DAY	3 / 8	BJ reads news clipping.
15	INT	WORLDVIEW CABLE - HALL OUTSIDE COOKIE'S	DAY	3 / 8	BJ debates with JIMMY.
12	INT	WORLDVIEW CABLE - STAGE	DAY	3 / 8	"Nobody liked Chip."
14	INT	WORLDVIEW CABLE - PLAYBACK CENTER	DAY	4 / 8	We meet KIM.
16	INT	WORLDVIEW CABLE - HALLWAY	DAY	2 2/8	They walk thru mayhem, cops arrive.
		--- END OF DAY 5 -- Fri, Jun 5, 1998 -- 6 7/8 pgs.			
11	INT	WORLDVIEW CABLE - CONTROL RM	DAY	3	BJ meets JIMMY.
17	INT	WORLDVIEW CABLE - CONTROL RM	DAY	6 / 8	JIMMY is arrested.
28	INT	WORLDVIEW CABLE - STAGE	DAY	2 1/8	CHIP is mad at JIMMY.
38	INT	WORLDVIEW CABLE - HALL OUTSIDE BATHROOM	DAY	1 / 8	MUMMY in toilet paper walks past BJ.
		--- END OF DAY 6 -- Sat, Jun 6, 1998 -- 6 pgs.			

```
-----------------------------------------------------------------
                         END OF WEEK #1
-----------------------------------------------------------------
```

51	INT	WORLDVIEW CABLE - STAGE	DAY	2 2/8	CHIP interviews DIRK.
52	INT	WORLDVIEW CABLE - CONTROL RM	DAY	4 / 8	CHIP is upset.
55	INT	WORLDVIEW CABLE - CONTROL RM	DAY	2 6/8	MITZI & CHIP have words.
		--- END OF DAY 7 -- Mon, Jun 8, 1998 -- 5 4/8 pgs.			

A SAMPLE OF A ONE-LINE SCHEDULE - FIGURE 7

The Production Budget

Once a line producer and director have prepared a shooting schedule that they both feel comfortable with, the line producer may then proceed to develop the other key tool for making the film: the production budget. This budget reflects *all* of the costs associated with taking the story from screenplay form, to preparations for filming (equipment, locations, manpower, etc.), to actual filming, and then to assembling the scenes in the film in the order in which director wishes to have an audience see it.

Production budgets can be as low as $200,000 which is generally the level of a high quality student film production, or as high as $100 million or more, which reflects the costs of a major studio action/adventure/visual effects film with a $20 million star actor. Production budgets can cost whatever someone wants it to cost or is willing to accept. Just remember that you usually get what you pay for!

It is at this point, the development of budget details, that some creative producers become intimidated as they are generally not as comfortable with budgets and numbers as line producers. However, it is relatively easy to translate a production schedule into a production budget with a little experience and a little help from a rate book.

For example, using a simplified schedule of 10 shooting days, it is safe to assume that a camera operator will be needed to run the camera for each of the 10 shooting days. If we know that a camera operator, who is a member of the cameraman's union, makes a minimum of $41.28 per hour, then we can begin to fill in one small piece of the budget pie.

The average shooting day is a 12 hour day. The first eight hours are worked at straight time and the 9th through the 12th hours are worked at time and one-half. Add 0.50 for a lunch period and you'll realize that the standard 12 hour work day is, in actuality, a 14.50 *pay* hours day. So, if the camera operator makes $41.28 per hour, then for a 12 hour *shoot* day, he will be paid $598.56. We have said that there are 10 shooting days. Therefore, the camera operator will be paid $5,985.60 for the 10 shooting days.

This same approach is used for all the members of the filming crew with slight variations based on the union to which the crew member belongs. As you can see, each day reflected on the shooting schedule can be translated into the dollar costs of manpower. It is the cumulative total of these numbers that creates the overall production budget for manpower. If you intend to produce a film with non-union labor, then the accounting can be even simpler, but the method is the same.

How does a line producer find out writer, director, actor and crew rates? And, how does he find out the rental rates for the filming equipment he will need to use during photography? This information is readily available in a variety of sources. Entertainment Partners (EP), a production services and payroll company, is one source. Each year this company publishes a three-ring binder (The EP Paymaster) that includes a detailed breakdown of the actors and crew members rates and working conditions as specified in their union contract. They even publish the same information in the book for other key filming cities such as New York, Chicago, San Francisco, and even British Columbia and Toronto, Canada. You can purchase The EP Paymaster for $55.00 by calling EP at 818-955-6299, or by ordering it through their internet site at www.ep-services.com.

To find out the rental rates of film equipment, a line producer can simply call one of the many vendors in Los Angeles and asks them for their rate sheets for the equipment that they rent. The rate sheet will show the standard rental rates for each piece of equipment. A line producer can use these rates when budgeting his equipment needs. However, a good line producer knows that when it comes time to actually renting the equipment, he will most likely be able to negotiate a better rate than the published rate.

Budgeting can be a time-consuming and tedious process, but nevertheless, an essential one. A line producer must consider a whole host of items beyond simply labor and equipment when budgeting his film. He must consider travel and housing needs, star entourage costs, weather conditions, and the laws covering the use of minors (children under the age of 18) to name just a few things. The more budgets a line producer prepares, experiences, and ultimately completes during principal photography, the more seasoned he will become with budgeting. The more cities for which he budgets a shooting schedule, and then actually ends up shooting in, the more knowledgeable about filming around the country he becomes. And, the more aware he becomes about the possibility for "glitches" between a planned budget and the actual costs that occur when problems arise.

The first page of a production budget is often called the Top-Sheet. The top-sheet summarizes all of the costs required to prepare, shoot and assemble the film for screening in a movie theater. An example of a top-sheet of a production budget is shown in Figure 8. As you can see, the production budget is split into three specific sections: above-the-line costs (ATL), below-the-line costs (BTL), and the total costs. ATL costs essentially reflect the creative aspects of the film including the

"WHO THE HELL IS CHIP GLASS"
Preliminary Working Budget

Exec Prods: Cielo Films, Inc.

Producers: Beth Dolan & Phil Nemy

Director: Luis Remesar

Budget Date: 11-26-97
Budget Draft: US Revision #1

Pre-Production: 1-12-98 (8 weeks)
Principal Photography: 3-9-98 (25 Days)
Post-Production: 4-7-98 (15 weeks)
Available: August 7, 1998
Location: Los Angeles
Unions: SAG

Script Date: 3-7-97

Acct#	Category Title	Page	Total
3100	STORY RIGHTS	1	$0
3200	WRITER	1	$51,600
3300	SCENARIO MISCELLANEOUS	1	$14,000
3500	RESIDUALS	1	$0
3600	PRODUCER	2	$287,500
3700	DIRECTOR	2	$91,100
3800	CAST	3	$270,800
3900	BITS & STUNTS	4	$114,570
	Total Fringes		$83,464
	TOTAL ABOVE-THE-LINE		$913,034
4200	EXTRAS & STANDINS	5	$69,383
4300	PRODUCTION STAFF	7	$232,029
4400	WARDROBE	9	$58,590
4500	MAKEUP & HAIRDRESSING	11	$33,038
4600	STILL CAMERA	11	$7,935
4700	CAMERA	12	$95,788
4800	PICTURE FILM & DAILIES	13	$91,498
4900	SET DRESSING	14	$62,900
5000	ACTION PROPS	15	$28,170
5100	ACTION PROPS - VEHICLES	15	$11,500
5200	MINIATURES	16	$0
5300	SET DESIGNING	16	$63,900
5400	SET CONSTRUCTION	17	$103,050
5500	SET STRIKE	18	$8,000
5600	VIDEO	19	$22,450
5700	SOUND - PROD RECORDING	20	$29,000
5800	SET LIGHTING	20	$71,940
5900	SET OPERATION	21	$79,560
6000	REHEARSALS	23	$700
6100	SPECIAL EFFECTS	23	$27,440
6200	TESTS	24	$15,000
6300	LOCATIONS	24	$146,768
6400	TRANSPORTATION	25	$198,526
	Total Fringes		$35,261
	TOTAL PRODUCTION		$1,492,426
6500	SECOND UNIT	30	$5,000
6700	PUBLICITY	30	$5,000
7000	SPECIAL PHOTO PROCESSES	31	$10,000
7100	PROJECTION	31	$12,625
7200	EDITING	31	$121,425
7300	TITLES	32	$10,000
7400	MUSIC	32	$30,000
7600	POST-PRODUCTION SOUND	33	$75,639
7700	SOUND FILM	34	$0
7900	FILM LAB EXPENSE	34	$59,216
8000	OPTICAL BLOW-UPS	34	$0
	Total Fringes		$0
	TOTAL POST PRODUCTION		$328,905
8500	INSURANCE & MEDICAL EXAMS	35	$52,900
8600	PURCHASE FILM FOOTAGE	35	$0
8800	LEGAL & MISCELLANEOUS	35	$135,450
8900	CERTIFICATES & ROYALTIES	35	$13,500
9000	FOREIGN VERSION DUB	35	$0
9100	STAGE RENTALS	36	$58,250
	Total Fringes		$0
	Total Other		$260,100
	TOTAL ABOVE-THE-LINE		$913,034
	TOTAL BELOW-THE-LINE		$2,081,431
	TOTAL ABOVE & BELOW-THE-LINE		$2,994,465
	GRAND TOTAL		$2,994,465

EXAMPLE OF A BUDGET TOP-SHEET - FIGURE 8

fees of the writers, producers, directors, actors, and casting director. The BTL costs are made up of three sub-sections: the shooting period, the completion period, and the other period.

The shooting period is the period when photography occurs. The completion period occurs after photography has been completed. During this period, the director and editor begin to assemble the film into a specific order in which to tell the story. At the same time, they begin working with the composer to create the music, the sound team to create the sound effects and dialogue tracks, the visual effects team to create the necessary visual effects, and so on. The completion period occurs when all the remaining elements come together to create the final film that will be sent to the theater for screening. The "other" period is not so much a period as it is a budget section. Included here are the costs for publicity, insurance, legal expenses and fringe benefits. All together, these three periods combined create the BTL.

The final section is simply the cumulative total of the ATL and BTL and is the total production budget. This is the number about which studios and independent investors are concerned. This number represents the investment required to make the film.

Choosing Your Collaborators

Investors and Studio Production Executives will be impressed with you if you have carefully considered certain specific personnel as your key collaborators. Being able to say who you wish to work with and why, as well as what you know about them from their last couple of films will indicate that you have done your homework. But how do you determine who is right for your film? While you're developing the schedule, you and the director should meet with potential candidates who will perform as your collaborators: the Production Designer, Director of Photography, Costume Designer, and Editor. These individuals will influence the look and feel of the visual aspects of the film. How do you determine who is right for the film? Research! The best way to determine who is the right person is to look at their films. Keep in mind that if the film you wish to make is comprised of mostly interior scenes, then you should look at the interior work of these specialists, not their exterior work, and visa versa.

Take, for example, the Production Designer. Once you've seen a few of the films that various Production Designers have worked on, you should be able to determine whose work you liked, whose sets and locations supported the story, rather than those that got in the way of telling the story. Once you have a few names, then check out these people. Call up the producers or production managers of the films you saw and ask them what the Production Designer was like to work with, did he finish the film on budget, did he come up with lots of creative ideas, does he like to build a lot of sets or can he work with most locations by dressing them up, is he arrogant, does he listen, etc. You'll be surprised how candid producers and production managers will be with you when they know you are considering using a particular designer with whom they have worked.

This same question and answer process should be used for determining which Director of Photography, Costume Designer and Editor you should use.

Producing Your Own Film

Rather than waiting around for a production company or motion picture studio to offer you an opportunity to produce a film and your director to direct one, or waiting for an agent to pick either of you up for representation, or even waiting for that agent to sell your names around town in the hope of securing a producing or directing job, why not make your own film? No, I'm not suggesting that you find $15 million dollars, hire Nicholas Cage to star, and start making your own feature-length motion picture (though if you have $15 million dollars, what are you waiting for?). What I am suggesting is that you either find or write a short film which can be made for a few thousand dollars. A short film is a film that generally runs no more than 40 minutes in length, has been shot with a non-union crew and often non-union actors, and is funded entirely from independent resources (i.e., parents, friends, co-workers, credit cards, etc.).

The success of the Sundance Film Festival, the Toronto Film Festival, the Houston Film Festival, and other festivals around the country, as well as the recent launching of the Independent Film Channel on television, is a strong commentary that independent filmmaking is thriving in North America. You don't have to have a lot of money these days to produce and direct an independent film. Major studios have subsidiaries who acquire and produce small independent films shot on shoe-string budgets. You can do this too, if you use a little common sense.

Independent Feature Project West

The Independent Feature Project West (IFP/W) is a not-for-profit organization created to help forge alliances between members of the independent community and collaborative artists, and to assist members with developing valuable creative and business contacts. If you are an independent producer or director , it is worth the annual membership price of $50. As a member, you will receive a monthly newsletter which shares news about the doings of current members, classified ads indicating film employment opportunities, a calendar of events including monthly screenings of independent films in current release, and advertisements for industry-related classes including screenwriting, the business of filmmaking, producer seminars with noted producers, and other seminars. Each month they also provide a Members Informal Get-Together at a local cafe, and an on-going breakfast series designed to give members one-on-one interaction and networking opportunities with agencies, producers, and studio executives.

One of the more important aspects of IFP/West is its library of resources and companies offering discounts to IFP/West members. For example, Eastman Kodak provides members who are producing or directing a film with a budget of $2.5 million or less with an 8% discount on Kodak film plus an additional 2% discount for cash purchases. The Studio Film & Tape Company in Hollywood offers members a 10% discount on Fuji film stocks. And on and on the list goes.

Panavision New Filmmakers Program

There are other resources you can take advantage of even if you are not a member of IFP/West. Panavision, the leading supplier of camera equipment to the motion picture industry, has established a program for the independent filmmaker called The New Filmmakers Program. You simply submit your film script to the Panavision office in Tarzana, CA and a committee at Panavision will read your script. If they believe that your script is a worthy representation of independent screenwriting, Panavision will provide you with a complete 16mm or Super 16mm camera package which you may use to shoot your film (subject to availability of course). They may even throw in a small lighting package as well. You must provide proof of insurance for the equipment to cover any loss or damage.

Other Independent Resources

The one item that filmmakers must always purchase is film raw stock. But this doesn't mean you have to purchase top of the line, new Kodak stock. Short ends, the unexposed film left over from completed film shoots that are sold to independent raw stock houses, are available in abundance and are usually sold at a significant discount.

Discounts and "freebies" can often be obtained if you are a student. While you may have just graduated from college or a university, you can become a "student" again by signing up for an extension course through the many college extension programs in Southern California. The class you sign up for may only be a one-day course, but you only need one day to run around town and purchase the film supplies you need using your student I.D.

Even the Screen Actors Guild will pitch in to help. If your film is being made as a "demo," meaning it is intended for film festivals only, and you agree that you will not charge admission to see it, then SAG will waive it's normal scale fee and allow its members to perform in the film. However, should you ever sell the film for a profit or charge an admission fee to see it, SAG will expect its members performing on camera to be appropriately compensated.

SHOWCASING YOUR
PRODUCING & DIRECTING WORK

We have already established that making a film is a collaborative art form. The producer needs the director as much as the director needs the producer. If either of you, producer and director, have ventured on and actually produced your film together, then you need to let the world know about it. To get the chance to produce another film, your first film needs exposure. And to get this exposure, you've got to "showcase" your work. Sounds like a catch-22, right? Well, actually it's not.

Showcasing your work means showing the town your talent by letting them see some of your work. Actors often do this by appearing in plays or readings. Writers do it by writing and producing their new plays, or presenting readings of their work. Producers and directors can do the same.

If you are not fortunate enough to have your film selected as a participant in one of the many film festivals, don't despair. You can create your own screening of your film. There are hundreds of screening rooms in Los Angeles available for rent at nominal fees. In fact, if you plead poverty to the screening room owner, you may even be able to get the room for free or on a deferred basis.

Once you've set up your screening, invite everyone you can to see your film. Send each person a postcard inviting them to the screening of your film. It doesn't matter if the people you are inviting can employ you or not, the idea is to get the room filled with as many industry professionals as you can. If any one of those people like your film, they may be willing to tell someone else that they have seen a terrific film, and that person may be able to employ you. See Figure 9 for a sample postcard.

Dear Mr. Smith,

You and a guest are cordially invited to a screening of my first production, a short film called "Making a Star", at the Director's Guild Screening Room on Friday September 13, 1998 at 8:00pm. The screening room is located at 1000 Sunset Blvd. in Hollywood. A reception will follow the screening.

Please call me at 818-555-1000 to make a reservation to insure that two good seats will be held for you.

Please join me for what I am certain will be a thoroughly enjoyable evening.

Sincerely,

I.M. Producer

Mr. John Smith
The Talent Agency
100 Anywhere St.
Los Angeles, CA 90038

EXAMPLE OF AN INVITATION TO SCREENING

FIGURE 9

Entering Your Film In Festivals

Film Festivals vary from the high-profile, Hollywood-attended Sundance Film Festival to the low profile, lesser known festivals such as the Aspen Film Festival. But don't underestimate the smaller festivals: they are equally as valuable. The key is to submit the film to as many festivals as you can, getting the film seen by as many people as you can. Don't worry about whether your film wins any awards. Most films don't. But then, many of the films that don't win awards do receive distribution deals.

The best way to approach submitting your film for competition in the festivals is to find out which festivals are looking for films like yours. And the easiest and fastest way to learn this is to call them. The Appendix of this book lists a number of the more prominent film festivals in the United States with their respective submission requirements and phone numbers. For a more comprehensive listing of festivals, purchase a copy of the *Guide to International Film and Video Festivals* by Kathryn Bowser. Published by the Foundation for Independent Video and Film, the book provides a detailed listing of all the current film festivals around the world, regardless of size or stature. A typical listing in her book would look something like this:

Sundance Film Festival
3619 Motor Avenue, Suite 240, Los Angeles, CA 90034
Tel: (310) 204-2091   Fax: (310) 204-3901
427 Main Street, Park City, UT 80460
Tel: (801) 645-7280   Fax: (801) 575-5175
Formats accepted: 35mm, 16mm, preview on 3/4" or 1/2"
Entry fee: $35 ($10 short film)
Month held: Late January
Deadline: Early November
Category: Independent
Contact: (In LA) Geoff Gilmore, programming director

99-Seat Waiver Theater

Another way you can showcase your talent is by producing live theater. Yes, *live* theater. Producing is producing, and either film or live theater showcase your producing and directing skills. Although Los Angeles is generally considered a film town, there is plenty of theater to be found. Over the last ten years, theater in Los Angeles has grown at a staggering rate. In 1987 there were about 50 live theaters. Today, there are over 100 theaters producing plays, musicals, readings, and other theatrical events. With this much theater, you can almost pick and choose with which theater group you'd like to be associated.

Producing and directing a scene, a staged reading, a one-act, or even a full-length play, is an excellent way to show the industry that you can do the work and that your work is interesting, entertaining, and exciting. It also shows that you know how to manage a production and, if it is a new, never-before-produced play, it says you know how to develop scripts and stories and present them in a theatrically entertaining fashion.

So let's assume that you and a director have worked together to produce and direct a brand new play in its world premiere and it garners rave reviews. Being the smart one that you are (and having read THE BASICS section of this book), you have sent letters and copies of the reviews to a variety of agents and studio executives, inviting them to see the show. If an agent is impressed by what he sees, he may want to meet both you and the director. He may even wish to represent both of you. Then he'll invite more studio production executives to the show to impress upon them that the agent has found a promising new producer and director talent team and they won't want to miss their show. That could lead you both to interviews with studio production executives and the possibility of reading a screen-play or two which just might be offered to both of you to produce and direct!

On the other hand, if a writer is impressed by what he sees, he may want to meet with both you and the director to tell you about a project he is writing that is having a few script problems. He may even let you read the script and ask for your input on how to fix it. That could lead to your reading the screenplay, giving the writer notes about what to change, and the writer loving what he hears. So the writer attaches both you and the director to the screenplay as the producer and director respectively, and you begin selling the script with your revised notes to the studios. A studio executive reads the screenplay and your notes, thinks that both you and the director are brilliant, and that leads to the executive offering the talent team the chance to produce and direct your first film!

As you can see by these two examples, working in the theater can act as a vehicle from which to launch your film career. So, how do you get the opportunity to produce or direct a play? Well, that goes back to the basics of finding the right script as we discussed earlier.

THE DIRECTOR

"BUT WHAT I REALLY WANT TO DO IS DIRECT!"

"Life in the movie business is like the beginning of a new love affair: it's full of surprises, and you are constantly getting fucked."

- from *Speed-the-Plow* by David Mamet

It's the classic Hollywood story. Two neophyte crew members are working together for the first time on a movie set and, in conversation, one crew member asks the other crew member, "What are you doing on the film?" The other crew member responds, "I'm a dolly grip, how about you?" The first crew member replies, "I'm a PA, but what I really want to do is direct!"

Almost all of the young talent you'll find on a film set, in a production office, or roaming a studio lot want to be directors. Why? Because as the Director, they believe they will have complete control of their film. Not so! If you believe that, then I have some well-watered land in Florida I want to sell you.

The Director may well be perceived as the individual who is in complete control of the film, while in reality, an individual investor, an investment group or studio that has put up the money, and to a certain degree, the producer, are the ones who are truly in control of the film. Remember the old saying about the Golden Rule? "He who has the gold makes the rules." Think about it: if you put up millions of dollars so a movie could be made, wouldn't you want to exercise significant control over how that money was spent? In Hollywood, money is the all important controlling factor. In other words, a Director is only as good as his last film: if it makes money, the Director will be given another film to direct, with plenty of, but not complete, freedom. But if the film flops, the Director may not see another directing opportunity for a long time.

Who Is Offered a Directing Job?

The key to finding work as a film director is in convincing someone in power that you know what you're doing. As with the producer, while it may sound trivial and simplistic, it is truly the key. Generally, a director will be offered the opportunity to direct a film because of one of the following reasons:

- he wrote the screenplay and will not allow it to be produced unless he directs it

- he worked with the screenwriter in developing the screenplay and has an oral or written agreement with the screenwriter that he will direct the screenplay

- he has directed at least one film before that the investor or studio executive has seen and liked

- he has directed at least one film before that the investor or studio executive has seen and liked, AND the film made money

- he has directed something (either a stage play, commercial, music video, documentary, etc.) that the investor or studio executive has seen and liked

- the studio owes the director a favor

- the director has a long-standing relationship with the investors or studio executives

If none of these applies in your case, then you have an even tougher task ahead of you. Still, you can be given a directing assignment simply on the basis that someone liked you, and believes that you know what you're talking about.

I have seen many a first-time director be given a chance to direct, when in fact, they know nothing about the craft. They simply impressed someone into believing that they understood the screenplay and could deliver it for a price. Why not go beyond this facade and prepare yourself - you'll find that more opportunities will be available if you truly know your craft.

THE MAKINGS OF A GOOD DIRECTOR

In my opinion it is more difficult finding work as a Director than it is as an Actor. On average, a film has roughly 25 speaking roles for which an Actor can be hired. However, each film has only one Director. The same ratios apply in television and stage plays. Therefore, a Director must fully know his craft before he ever attempts to find work as a film director.

Just as with the producer, there is no exact science to finding a directing job in the film business. Everyone gets their first break in their own unique way. Some never get their chance. But since there are so few opportunities out there, you'll increase the odds in your favor by being light-years ahead of the competition by being well prepared. How? By developing and mastering the specific tools and skills of the director to which many of the competition don't pay attention.

In the two previous sections entitled THE WRITER and THE PRODUCER, I illustrated the collaborative process of screenplay development between the writer, producer and director. I explained the three primary tools of the trade: an idea, a story and a screenplay. Nothing can happen unless a writer, producer or director have a screenplay. I examined how to find, develop and pitch the screenplay. I even detailed the collaboration with the producer during pre-production. Finally, I showed how the producer and director must work together to market or showcase their film. *So, if you skipped THE WRITER and THE PRODUCER sections, I suggest you go back now and read them.* Then we can come back and deal with finding a screenplay, and that means finding a writer.

Finding a Writer

If you are not confident in your own writing skills, talk to a few writers you may know and ask them if they would be interested in helping you "flesh out" or develop your own story. As I said earlier, producers and directors are not expected to write screenplays. On the contrary, that is why they hire writers! You should know, however, that in the medium of television, most producers are also the show's writers. But in film, the producer and director have the luxury of not having to write the scripts themselves. All they must do is read them and determine if they work. But in order to do this, a director and producer must have a screenplay to read, and if they have no relationships with writers, then how do they get screenplays to read?

There is no right or wrong way to obtaining screenplays, but here are a few suggestions as to how you can develop relationships with writers so that you may read their work before anyone else does:

- Talk to people. Tell everyone you meet that you are a director looking for screenplays and inquire as to whether they are writers or know of any writers who might allow you to read their work. You'd be surprised how many people write screenplays or have friends who are working on screenplays.

- Advertise. There are a number of film industry trade papers in which a director can place an advertisement seeking screenplays. *Backstage West/Dramalogue, Daily Variety,* and *The Hollywood Reporter* are just a few of the many trade papers. But keep in mind that you want your notice to appear in trades that are read by writers. If you don't know which ones those are, try contacting the Samuel French Bookshops in both Los Angeles and New York and ask for their help with the names and addresses of trades which allow advertisements for screenplays wanted.

- Attend Seminars. Sign up for a few of the screen-writing seminars where you'll get a chance to meet and talk with beginning writers. Take an active interest in their work and ask to read it. Offer your criticism only if they ask for it. Who knows, maybe some of your comments will help them to better understand where their screenplay is not working and they may be so impressed that they will be willing to work on the script with you guiding it as the director!

- Purchase a Writers Directory. The WGAw, like most unions, publishes a directory of the members once a year which lists addresses, phone numbers, representation contacts and screenplay credits on every member of the union. You can purchase a copy of the directory from the WGAw or you can buy it at most industry bookshops such as Samuel French for $25. Once you have it, read through and familiarize yourself with the many writers in the union. Note their credits. If any credit suggests to you that their style of writing might be best suited for ideas that you may have, contact the writer and pitch them your idea. If they like the idea, they may be willing to work on it with you. But don't take a "no" personally. It may not be what the writer had in mind to work on. You can always contact him again with another story idea.

Once you have found a writer who will help you develop your screenplay, or even has a screenplay of his own which interests you, a good director must be able to read a writer's script and discern whether it is good or bad writing. As a director, you will not always have the luxury of developing your own ideas. More often than not, you'll have to interpret a writer's words to tell the story as you, the director, see it. If you don't have the ability to determine a good story from a bad one, you'll end up investing valuable time and energy on a project that was hopeless from the start. This, too, is a skill that can be learned and mastered with practice.

With screenplay in hand, you may think that all you need to do now is to sell yourself and the screenplay to someone willing to finance it as a film. Yes, it is true, you can begin to start selling. But at this point, why not insure your success by doing the necessary homework on the fundamentals of directing.

DOING YOUR HOMEWORK

As I've already stated, the fastest way to be given a job directing a motion picture is to have a marketable screenplay. As much as 90% of your day should be spent in selling that screenplay to anyone and everyone who will listen. The other 10% is spent in preparing yourself to begin employment as a director. You can start by familiarizing yourself with the primary tools the director must fully understand before he is prepared to step onto a film set.

A good director needs to understand the basics of cinematography, production design, costume design, and editing. He needn't be a master of any one of these as he will be supported by experts in those areas. Nevertheless, a director should have a very good working knowledge of two key production elements: the motion picture camera and the film editing process.

The Camera

The camera is a complex and precise tool which must be fully understood by the director if he expects it to photograph the images he seeks. The Director's best friend is the camera. It can help him support a weak performance by an actor, create a mood, provide excitement, and ultimately tell his story. Essentially, there are six key ingredients to using a camera: camera movement, light, filters, lenses, lens stop, and film stock. And the director must be conversant with them all.

The movement of the camera may sound trivial, but it can affect the entire emotion and heart of the scene. A director must know when it is appropriate to use a crane to swing the camera in and around the action of the scene, or when to use a steadicam apparatus to create a fluid and smooth camera movement. Knowing when to move the camera and knowing how its movement adds or detracts to a scene is crucial.

Light will affect the image seen through the camera. Natural light can create a different mood than artificial light. It can also change the color of set pieces and wardrobe, as well as the color and age of an actor's face. A director may even choose to use both natural and artificial light simultaneously to create a specific desired effect.

Color filters can be used to enhance or diminish the quality of the light. A blue filter used against an already blue sky may make the sky come even more alive, making a statement that a director may desire. An amber filter may lend an "old world" sepia glow to the images, creating a warm romantic setting for a love scene. Filters can even be used to balance light. When filming in a sports arena, sodium lighting is often used to flood the large space with light, but it also provides a subtle blueness to the interior. A director may use a filter to balance this blueness so that the light on the actors' faces looks more appealing.

Camera lenses come in a variety of sizes and a director must know which one to use in order to establish a desired mood. Currently, lenses being used in the film industry range in size from 9 millimeters to over 600 millimeters. These lenses can be separated into three basic groups: wide-angle lenses, mid-range lenses and long lenses.

Wide-angle lenses (from 9mm to 21 mm) often distort the picture. Therefore, it's safe to say that the wider then lens, the greater the distortion. With wide-angle lenses, objects seem farther apart. The distortion is also noticeable with vertical lines. They seem to be forced closer together at the top of the frame.

Wide-angle lenses also have a greater focal depth of field. The focal depth is defined by J. Kris Malkiewicz, in his book *Cinematography: A Guide for Film Makers and Film Teachers,* as the distance through which objects will appear sharp in front of and behind the point at which the camera is focused.

Long lenses (generally 50mm and larger) compress or squeeze the space. If you line up a few objects starting in the foreground and moving away from the camera towards the background, then, through a long lens the objects will seem to be closer together. So it is safe to say that the longer the lens, the closer the objects seem, both to the camera and to one another. A good example of the use of long lenses can be found in many of the scenes from films shot in San Francisco involving automobile chases. You might want to view the films "Bullitt" or "The Rock" to fully appreciate what I mean.

There are still another set of lenses commonly used that come closest to the vision of the human eye. These lenses are referred to as the mid-range lenses (generally from 28 mm to 40 mm).

The lens stop, which determines the amount of light that passes through the lens onto the film stock, is very important. The lens stop is created by opening or closing an iris placed in the lens. "Open the stop", letting in more light by setting the iris in its most open position, or "Stop down", closing the iris so it allows the least amount of light to reach the film, can often be heard as a command from the Director of Photography to the Camera Assistant as the shot is being lit.

Film Stock and Film Formats

Knowing the ins and outs of a camera is important. Knowing about what goes inside the camera is just as important. I'm sure you realize that you put film into the camera. The real question is, do you know what kind of film to put in the camera? Once again, you don't need to be an expert when it comes to film sizes, emulsions and speeds, but it certainly helps. And it also says you know a little something about cameras, which is a good thing since it is the primary electro-mechanical tool you'll need to make your film!

In today's filmmaking world, there are a number of film sizes to choose from including 8mm, Super 8mm, 16mm, Super 16mm, 35mm, Super 35mm, and 65mm which is often referred to as 70mm. Super 8mm and 8mm, although very grainy and almost amateurish in their look, are becoming a more popular creative choice for directors. Look at the films "Natural Born Killers" and "Private Parts" as prime examples of how effective this primitive film stock can be.

The film stock of choice for documentary filmmaking tends to be 16mm because it is significantly cheaper than 35mm and the majority of 16mm cameras are smaller and lighter to carry. Since documentary filmmaking can often require lots of hand-held camera work, this becomes an important factor.

Super 16mm is being used more frequently in the independent filmmaking world and in episodic television production. For example, Robert Young's film "The Ballad of Gregorio Cortez" was shot on Super 16mm. So was the CBS television series "Dr. Quinn, Medicine Woman." You probably would not have guessed this had I not told you. The difference is almost imperceptible on *television,* and Super 16mm costs a lot less than 35mm. So, in this case it is a smart financial decision to use Super 16mm.

But the decisions are not always economic ones. Super 16mm provides a grainier print than 35mm, and the increased graininess is much more noticeable in motion picture film than in television. In addition, one must "print up" the Super 16mm to 35mm in order to release the film for viewing in large theaters around the country which can potentially add costs. Incidentally, the references to a "print" and "print up" do not mean the hard copy photographic print one gets back from the local drug store after dropping off a roll of film for next day developing. In the motion picture industry, a "print" is a roll of movie film that has been generated from the film negative and is projected onto a screen for audience viewing.

The standard film stock for shooting motion pictures today is 35mm. It would be safe to say that nine films out of ten which are screened in large theaters around the country (often referred to as "theatrically released") are shot on 35mm. Why? Because it provides the best image for the price and it is available in a variety of film speeds. Not to mention that most theaters around the country don't cary 16mm projectors.

Even knowing that 35mm is the standard shooting film stock, you would further set yourself apart from the competition if you know the whys and whens of using Super 35mm instead of 35mm film stock. Super 35mm was created as an alternative to 35mm as a way of providing the filmmaker with a wide screen or "Cinemascope" image without having to use anamorphic lenses (lenses which squeeze and distort the image).

Ever notice when watching a film in a theater that the projection screen is noticeably wider than normal? You might have noticed this if you saw Kevin Costner's film "Dances With Wolves" in the theater. His film was projected on a wider screen than the normal 35mm screen. This type of wider screen image can be achieved in one of two ways: anamorphic and Super 35.

To further examine film formats, I've chosen to use a portion of the best report on the subject that I have found, *Pros and Cons of Film Formats* by Robert C. Hummel. Information from this report is reprinted below by permission from the American Society of Cinematographers:

The most common method, called anamorphic 2.35:1 (or 2.40:1), is achieved by using an anamorphic lens during filming to squeeze the visual image so that it fits into the normal area between the 35mm perforations. When the final print is theatrically released and shown in theaters, an anamorphic lens is also used on the film projector to widen the image so that it will appear as it was originally composed. Since this technique, shown in Figure 10, entails the not inconsequential expense of using anamorphic lenses during filmmaking *and* the film screening, a less expensive method was developed, called Super 35mm.

In shooting with Super 35mm film stock, normal lenses are used, so the visual image is not distorted on the film itself. Figure 11 illustrates this. However, to create a release print from the Super 35mm negative (so that is can be shown in theaters), a process similar to that of anamorphic 2.35:1 must be used: an interpositive print of the film is squeezed to conform to a standard anamorphic frame, from which an anamorphic frame internegative is created. When the final print is screened, it must be projected through an anamorphic lens so that it will appear as it was originally composed. The savings occurs in cutting out

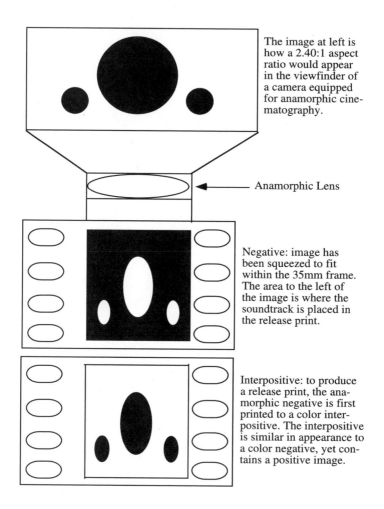

The image at left is how a 2.40:1 aspect ratio would appear in the viewfinder of a camera equipped for anamorphic cinematography.

Anamorphic Lens

Negative: image has been squeezed to fit within the 35mm frame. The area to the left of the image is where the soundtrack is placed in the release print.

Interpositive: to produce a release print, the anamorphic negative is first printed to a color interpositive. The interpositive is similar in appearance to a color negative, yet contains a positive image.

ANAMORPHIC 2.40:1 PROCESS

FIGURE 10
(continued on next page)

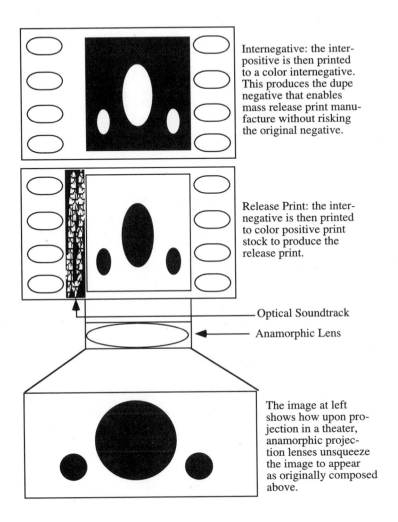

Internegative: the inter-
positive is then printed
to a color internegative.
This produces the dupe
negative that enables
mass release print manu-
facture without risking
the original negative.

Release Print: the inter-
negative is then printed
to color positive print
stock to produce the
release print.

Optical Soundtrack

Anamorphic Lens

The image at left
shows how upon pro-
jection in a theater,
anamorphic projec-
tion lenses unsqueeze
the image to appear
as originally composed
above.

ANAMORPHIC 2.40:1 PROCESS

FIGURE 10
(continued from previous page)

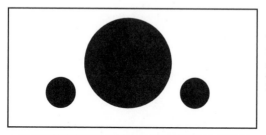

The iamge at left is how a 2.40:1 aspect ratio would appear in the viewfinder of a camera equipped for Super 35 cinematography.

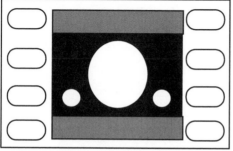

Negative: Super 35 is a full aperture format. This means the entire frame is exposed with image information, including the area normally reserved for the soundtrack (in all of these illustrations, the area not used by the 2.40 composition has been shaded). The desired aspect ratio is achieved by masking off information above and below the 2.40:1 composition.

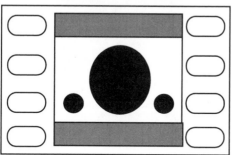

Interpositive: to produce a release print, the full aperture negative is first printed to a color interpositive. The interpositive is similar in appearance to a color negative, yet contains a positive image.

SUPER 35 PHOTOGRAPHIC PROCESS

FIGURE 11
(continued on next page)

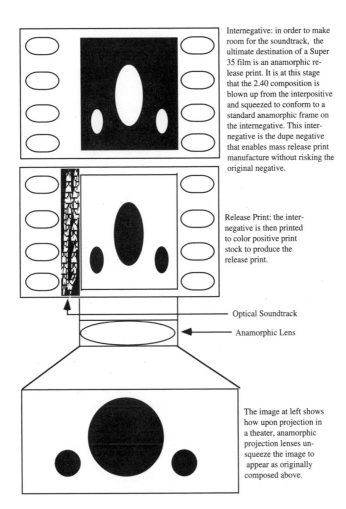

Internegative: in order to make room for the soundtrack, the ultimate destination of a Super 35 film is an anamorphic release print. It is at this stage that the 2.40 composition is blown up from the interpositive and squeezed to conform to a standard anamorphic frame on the internegative. This internegative is the dupe negative that enables mass release print manufacture without risking the original negative.

Release Print: the internegative is then printed to color positive print stock to produce the release print.

Optical Soundtrack

Anamorphic Lens

The image at left shows how upon projection in a theater, anamorphic projection lenses unsqueeze the image to appear as originally composed above.

SUPER 35 PHOTOGRAPHIC PROCESS

FIGURE 11
(continued from previous page)

the use of anamorphic lenses during the filming process.

The down-side of shooting Anamorphic 2.35 can be seen with close-ups. Single close-ups result in widened areas on either side of a face. Objects which would otherwise appear as part of the background now have the potential to appear as distractions in the foregroud. Often this format can require building wider sets which can negatively impact a construction budget. And as with a wider format, crowd scenes generally require more background extras to fill the shot, potentially adding money to your budget.

65mm is used quite often for "epic" or "landscape drama" films. An example of this would be Cecil B. DeMille's film "Ben Hur" as well as Ron Howard's film "Far And Away." Filming in 65mm is not done often because it is expensive. A specially made camera must be used to house the film which is almost twice the size of standard 35mm film stock. Since it is such a large format, it is the choice for most Visual Effects Photographers because a larger piece of film creates a large palate on which to create effects. 65mm negatives are actually printed onto 70mm stock.

So now you know a little bit about film stocks. But believe you me, there's a heck of a lot more to know. For example, which speed of film do you use when? When is it most appropriate to use Eastman Kodak 5296 film? What effect does 5247 film stock have on low light situations? There are so many more quesetions about this subject, it is staggering! But don't be intimidated. Learn as much as you can and you'll impress the heck out of everyone, but don't feel you need to be an expert - your director of photography can help you when it comes to rolling the camera. Meanwhile, it's important to learn a little something about aspect ratios as it will directly affect your final product.

Aspect Ratios

Aspect ratios refer to the varying ratio of the width to height dimensions of the image you see in the viewing frame. The most prevalent aspect ratios used in the U.S. today are 1.85 and 2.35, spoken as "One Eight Five" and "Two Three Five." The numbers 1.85 and 2.35 are determined by dividing the width of the picture by the height of the picture. You may see them written as 1.85:1 and 2.35:1, but it means the same thing. Figure 12 illustrates the aspect ratios we will discuss here.

Deciding which format to use is not just a technical question. It is as important a creative question as a technical one. Comedy, drama, action/adventure, and all other genres can be shot in both formats. But there are pros and cons to both. Having the knowledge of the pros and cons will help you to make the best decision for your film. And it will help illustrate to your colleagues that you know a thing or two about the filmmaking process. Let's take a quick look at the advantages to both formats.

The industry standard film format is "One Eight Five" (1.85). Nine times out of ten, as an audience member, you're probably watching a film which is screening in a 1.85 format. 1.85 tends to be a more intimate format. It is often used with interior photography work and it gives you a greater depth of field. Almost any 35mm camera will accommodate this format making it the most financially reasonable choice. The downside of shooting 1.85 is the negative itself. Because the image area is small, the 1.85 image tends to be grainier than 2.35. The negative area of 2.35 is 59% greater than that of 1.85. 1.85 has a greater height to it, which means that the ceilings of sets are more apt to be photographed. This can restrict the way the cameraman may light the set.

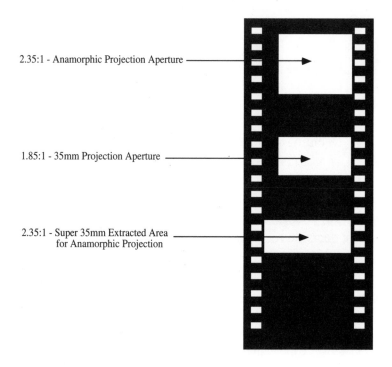

2.35:1 - Anamorphic Projection Aperture

1.85:1 - 35mm Projection Aperture

2.35:1 - Super 35mm Extracted Area
for Anamorphic Projection

ASPECT RATIOS

FIGURE 12

As you can see, knowing and understanding the camera, film raw stock and aspect ratio formats will make you a better prepared director. Wouldn't it be nice to have everyone impressed with the fact that you were ready and well prepared when your first big chance came along? But once you've shot your film and it's "in the can," what do you do next? You start editing (by the way, "in the can" is a slang term which means the film has been exposed and returned to the can from whence it came - it is then sent to the processing lab for development).

Film Editing

It has been said that renowned silent film director D.W. Griffith shot most of his films "off the cuff," shooting a certain amount of film of the same scene from different angles and levels of close-ups (often called "coverage") which allowed him enough footage to experiment with the material when he came to edit it. However, today, with the cost of making films reaching exorbitant levels, directors must be more judicious in the shots they plan. You might even say that when shooting a film, one should "shoot to edit."

A director can help himself long before ever exposing one frame of film by *story-boarding* the entire screenplay. Story-boarding is the process of telling the story through a series of hand-drawn pictures that illustrate the action, camera angles and transitions from shot to shot. Essentially, the storyboard is a blueprint of the entire film, laid out with simplistic and rough editorial choices. The storyboard can be changed, altered, and refined as many times as need be before the camera ever starts rolling. The story-boarding process can help a director and editor lay out basic editorial choices ahead of time, thereby saving valuable time on the set for camera set-ups, and decreasing the budget.

A director must have a strong working knowledge of the process of editing. While he may have made choices during photogrpahy about the way to shoot the sceens (long, medium, close-up and extreme close-up shots, pans, fades, etc.), he must now determine the best way to assemble that footage in a manner that will tell his story dramatically. This is called film editing and is the domain of the Film Editor. However, the overall film is the responsibility and vision of the director. Obviously, then, the director and editor share a close relationship when it comes to telling the story. In fact, a director often relies heavily on his editor to help him structure the story in an exciting, visually interesting, and emotionall gripping fashion.

Good editing can make a good film better, save a bad performance by an actor, and even influence the box office. It can help enhance the emotion and pacing of the film. On the other hand, bad editing can kill what started out as a good film. It can throw off the fluidity of the story and bore the audience. Good editing is a combination of pacing, emotion, action, and drama all created by splicing film scenes together in an order which will evoke these elements. Since this is not a book about "how to edit," I will assume that you, the reader, already know the basics of film editing. If you don't, stop reading now, run to a bookstore and pick up a copy of a "how to edit film" book such as "The Technique of Film Editing" by Karel Reisz and Gavin Miller.

With the advent of computer technology, film editing can now be supported by electronic tools. Lightworks™ and Avid™ are just a couple of the available electronic and digital editing tools available to a director today. While not cheap, electronic editing can provide a director with a greater number of editorial choices in a much shorter time span than traditional film editing techniques, which may ultimately shorten the editing process, potentially saving money. As a director, one should become conversant in as many electronic editing techniques as possible. For information about taking a class to learn how to use these electronic editing systems, check the Appendix of this book for a complete list of editing system companies and post-production houses.

The more research, education and knowledge a director has about these and other areas, the better able he will be in establishing his overall vision for the film, and at the same time create a stronger communication link with his colleagues by speaking their language.

WORKING WITH ACTORS

Although it is important for a director to fully under-stand and master the tools of directing such as aspect ratios, cameras, film stock, and the like, the greatest skill of a director is his successful relationship with his actors. The best directors are those who are former actors. While a director doesn't have to be Laurence Olivier himself, if he has at least studied and tried acting and has understood the basics of the craft, he is more apt to communicate intellectually and emotionally the heart of a character and/or scene to an actor. The more conversant a direc-tor is about various acting techniques, the better his chances are at getting an actor to respond to his understanding of the scene. A director must also create a comfortable, trusting environment on the set in which actors can work. If actors feel the environ-ment and people in it are supporting their work, they are more apt to take risks for their director which may lead to stronger, more interesting performances.

While working on finding and developing a screenplay, or writing your own, a good director will keep working with actors. After you've directed three or four films, you'll no longer need to continually keep brushing up on these skills. But while you're starting out, do it. It's important for a couple of reasons:

- it keeps your creative juices flowing. As long as you are working on scripts with actors, then you're using your creativity. Out of creativity comes ideas, and from ideas come stories. Maybe one of those stories will be good enough to be bought.

- you never know when one of the actors you're working with will become a star. Stars can be influential over who will direct them. If you've a good working relationship with the actor who has become a star, they may be able to help you get your first film directing job. This is a good example of networking at its best.

THE DIRECTORS GUILD OF AMERICA

In an earlier section of this book, I covered "The Basics," those factors common to all the players in the film industry. But there are some aspects of the Director's union that need to be touched upon for your benefit, such as how to get into the Director's union.

Getting Into the DGA

The DGA represents Directors, Unit Production Managers (UPM), Assistant Unit Production Managers (AUPM), 1st, 2nd and 2nd 2nd Assistant Directors (ADs), and DGA Trainees. Probably 90% of the productions in Los Angeles are staffed by DGA personnel. In general, the really low budget productions (films with production budgets of $1,000,000 or less) are generally staffed with non-DGA labor. All of the major studios are signatory to the DGA and as such are required to use DGA labor, regardless of budget size.

How does one become a DGA member? First you should know that the DGA is more open to the idea of new members when the majority of their membership are working, than they are when the majority is unemployed. Nevertheless, there are two ways to get into the DGA: by applying to the DGA Contract Administration Office and meeting the prerequisites, or through the Assistant Director's Training Program.

Applying To The DGA

In Los Angeles, there are two Membership Rosters to which one can apply for acceptance: The Southern California Roster and the 3rd Area Roster. The Southern California Roster covers all of Southern California, from Santa Barbara south to San Diego. The 3rd Area Roster covers all the other areas of the United States except New York City and State, and Southern California.

To qualify for the Southern California Roster, a prospective member must have been employed a minimum of 400 days as a 2nd 2nd AD, 2nd AD, 1st AD or UPM on a non-union motion picture or television production. 25% of the 400 days must be pre-production days and 75% of the 400 days must be shooting days.

To qualify for the 3rd Area Roster, a prospective member must have been employed a minimum of 120 days as a 2nd 2nd AD, 2nd AD, 1st AD or UPM on a non-union motion picture or television production. 25% of the 120 days must be pre-production days and 75% of the 120 days must be shooting days.

Keep in mind that days worked as a Set Production Assistant or Key Set Production Assistant will not be accepted as worked days towards eligibility on either the Southern California or 3rd Area Rosters. Once an applicant has been accepted into the DGA and is listed on the 3rd Area Roster, he can then apply for the Southern California Roster once he has worked the required 400 days in an AD capacity.

For either Roster, proof of these worked days must be submitted to the DGA Contract Administration Office (DGACA) which is a division of the Association of Motion Picture & Television Producers (AMPTP). The *minimum paperwork* they need to see for proof of each day the applicant has worked as an AD is as follows:

- copy of the applicant's deal memo. It is usually a one-page form detailing the working conditions and pay scale the applicant is given on the production. Usually the applicant signs the deal memo the first day he begins employment on a production.

- copy of the I-9 Form with back-up documentation. The I-9 is required by the Immigration & Naturalization Office of the US government to prove the applicant is an American citizen.

• copies of paychecks or pay stubs

• copies of call sheets and production reports

• copies of staff and crew lists

• copies of any production memorandums prepared by the applicant during production

Once this paperwork is submitted to the DGACA, it will be reviewed and a recommendation will be made to the DGA UPM/1st AD Committee. The DGA UPM/1st AD Committee is comprised of active UPM and 1st AD members of the DGA who have volunteered their time to review all DGA membership applications. They have 30 days in which to review the application and make their findings known to the DGACA. If they vote to reject the application, they will tell the DGACA the areas where they feel the applicant must strengthen and improve his skills.

The DGACA will notify the applicant of the outcome. The applicant can then re-apply after three months or whenever the applicant has met the additional requirements set forth by the DGA UPM/1st AD Committee.

If the Committee votes to accept the application, then the applicant is offered membership in the DGA at the appropriate level (1st or 2nd AD). The applicant must then pay his initiation fee (currently $5,138 for 1st AD's and $3,444 for 2nd AD's) and his name is placed on the 3rd Area Availability Roster. This is because all new members must first begin working in the 3rd Area before being eligible for work in either the New York area or Southern California area. The Roster is available to anyone in the film industry who requests it so that they can see who is available for work. This will mean that the "new member" can now be hired to perform DGA AD work anywhere in the US except in New York City & State and Southern California.

Current membership dues for the DGA are paid quarterly. The dues are $50.00 per quarter plus $1.5% of your DGA earnings.

The Assistant Directors Training Program

The other way one can gain entrance into the DGA is through the Assistant Directors Training Program. The Assistant Directors Training Program was set up as a joint effort by the DGA and the AMPTP to ensure the proper training of 2nd AD's. How do you get into the program? Well, that's easier said than done.

The Assistant Directors Training Program is an intensely competitive one. Over 2500 individuals apply to the program each year. Application forms are available in mid-September and will be mailed to interested parties by writing to The Assistant Directors Training Program (see Appendix for address). The applications are screened and roughly 1000 of the applicants are invited to participate in the first phase of the application process, a written examination. Before testing begins, each applicant must pay a non-refundable $50.00 testing fee.

The test is given once a year in Los Angeles & Chicago, usually between February and April. The written examination *does not* test the applicants knowledge of the film industry, but rather consists of a battery of tests that assess job related skills such as verbal, reasoning, mathematical abilities, organization and interpersonal skills. Some people have recommended that reviewing the high school SAT testing book is a good refresher for what one may find on The Assistant Directors Training Program test.

Based on evaluation of test scores and written applications, the most promising candidates are invited for group and individual interviews with the Screening and Admissions Committee. The interviews are held only in Los Angeles, usually in Spring or Summer. The final selection is based on test scores, and group and individual interviews. Not more than twenty people are accepted into the program, sometimes as few as five!

Acceptance in the program does not mean the applicant is instantly a DGA member, nor does it mean he will graduate from the Program. If an applicant is accepted, however, the DGA expects him to make a commitment to finishing the Program in it's entirety. Over the next two to three years, he will be assigned to work on a variety of productions in film and television as a DGA Trainee. The Trainee position is a paying one with current wages set at:

1st 100 days worked	$392/wk plus OT
2nd 100 days worked	$421/wk plus OT
3rd 100 days worked	$451/wk plus OT
4th 100 days worked	$482/wk plus OT

After the Trainee has completed 400 days of work as a DGA Trainee, the DGA will offer the Trainee membership into the union. Upon payment of your AD initiation fees, The Trainee is promoted to 2nd AD status and his name is added to the Southern California Roster. Once on the Southern California Roster, a member is able to work in both the Southern California area as well as the 3rd Area.

The Prepared Director

At this point, you have a screenplay you're ready to sell with you attached as a director. You've done your homework and know exactly how you would shoot the film and who you would employ as your collaborators assuming you could find financing for the film. Now it's time to get out there and let everyone know about your project through networking.

BEHIND THE CAMERA

THE CREW

"The movie business is the only business in the world where the assets go home at night."

- attributed to Dorothy Parker

Let's take a look at what various people actually do during the course of making a film so that we can determine which position interests you. First I need to explain that it is standard practice in the film industry to divide the positions involved in producing a film as either "Above The Line" (ATL) or "Below The Line" (BTL) personnel (additional information about the ATL & BTL can be found on page 152). These designations come from the financial, budgeting and accounting format of each film. ATL personnel are considered "non-controllable" or variable costs and are generally the "creative members" of the team such as the Writer, Producer, Director, and Cast.

The BTL personnel are considered "controllable" or fixed costs and are generally the Technicians or Crew such as the Costume Designer, Production Designer, Director of Photography, etc.

I will define all of the ATL & BTL positions so you'll have a better idea of each person's function on a film. Those positions in **bold type** are considered heads of their respective departments. The order in which they are listed is the order in which they are often found in a film budget.

ATL POSITIONS

WRITER - hired to write the screenplay.

> • WRITER'S ASSISTANT/SECRETARY - assists the writer with story research and helps prepare script changes by typing them into a script writing program in the computer; sends script changes to all the people on the film who need to know that a change has been made. Usually this person is off the payroll long before the cameras start rolling.

PRODUCER - the first person involved on a film project and the last person off the completed project. Producers are often given a variety of titles which can help indicate just what their role on the film will truly be. The creative producer, often given the sole "Produced By" credit on a film, traditionally finds and develops a script; he arranges for the film's financing, then hires the writers, director and actors. His involvement often continues through the theatrical release of the film. The creative producer can be equated to the Chief Executive Officer of a company - the buck stops with him.

LINE PRODUCER - often given a "Co-Producer" or "Executive Producer" credit on a film. The line producer functions more like a Chief Operating Officer, managing the day-to-day operation of the film company. He supervises both ATL and BTL personnel during production, working side-by-side and in partnership with the creative producer. The line producer is the nuts-and-bolts man who must supervise and approve the scheduling, budgeting, and cost reporting of the entire production. Generally, the Line Producer's employment ends with the completion of photography. However, if he possesses experience and skill in the area of post-production, a Line Producer can often be employed until the theatrical release of the film in order to supervise the post-production process.

The "Produced By" screen credit is a coveted perk. When a film is awarded a "Best Picture" Academy Award, an Oscar is given ONLY to those individuals who have obtained a screen credit of ***"Produced By" or "Producer."*** An Executive Producer, Co-Producer, or any other variation of a "producing" credit will not result in an Oscar should the film win an Academy Award.

- ASSISTANT TO THE PRODUCER - assists the producer with personal and clerical responsibilities.

- ASSOCIATE PRODUCER - title varies from film to film. It can be given to the Line Producer's 2nd in command, the Creative Producer's 2nd in command, a Unit Production Manager when a Line Producer credit is not available, the Financiers, an Agent, and sometimes a Personal Manager; most often given to someone who performs the role of the Post-Production Supervisor.

DIRECTOR - ultimately responsible for all the creative aspects of the film.

- ASSISTANT TO THE DIRECTOR - personal assistant to the Director, handling everything from personal tasks (scheduling meetings, making phone calls, getting lunch, etc.) to film research and story notes.

- SECOND UNIT DIRECTOR - in charge of directing sequences not involving principal actors; often Stunt Coordinators are hired as 2nd Unit Directors.

- STORYBOARD ARTIST - draws on paper or on a computer the action of the scenes in sequences under the supervision of the Director; is usually hired during pre-production and laid-off during principal photography.

CASTING DIRECTOR - interviews actors, recommends them to the director, then hires them and negotiates their contracts; works under supervision of the Director and Producer.

STUDIO TEACHER/WELFARE WORKER - in charge of following and maintaining the strict rules governing the working conditions of minors (child actors). Studio Teachers function as school teachers, insuring that child actors continue their education even though they are outside of their normal school and classroom.

STUNT COORDINATOR - organizes and coordinates all stunts, insuring safety of the cast and crew that are involved in the stunts.

CAST - principal actors in the film.

BITS - supporting actors in the film.

EXTRAS/ATMOSPHERE - actors without lines and without significant action in the scene, whose job it is to fill the background of a scene lending a sense of realism to the action.

BTL POSITIONS

UNIT PRODUCTION MANAGER - (UPM) also referred to as production manager, the Producer's right-hand person on the film; coordinates and supervises all administrative, financial and technical details of the production; oversees the activities of the BTL, and often the ATL, for the line producer. After a UPM has worked extensively in this position, he can usually be employed as a Line Producer, taking on a more elevated role in the making of the film. Good UPM's are in high demand.

- PRODUCTION OFFICE COORDINATOR - (POC) a clerical member of production staff who reports to the UPM as his right-hand; liaison between the production office and all other groups during production; supervises the production office staff. A good POC is worth his weight in gold!

- ASSISTANT PRODUCTION OFFICE COORDI-NATOR - (APOC) the POC's right hand; supervises the Office Production Assistants.

- <u>PRODUCTION SECRETARY</u> - usually responsible for preparing and distributing script rewrites which occur during filming; handles clerical duties assigned by the POC; generally comes on payroll after the writer's assistant is off payroll.

- <u>OFFICE PRODUCTION ASSISTANT</u> - (PA) the labor force of the production office; reports directly to the POC; assigned to most menial tasks (picking up lunches, making coffee, making copies, answering phones, etc.); nicknamed the "gofer" which refers to the task of "going for" various items; i.e, pickups/ deliveries.

1ST ASSISTANT DIRECTOR - the Director's right-hand; liaison between Director and UPM; keeps the production moving; supervises the Extras; maintains the call time; maintains order and discipline on the set; tells the Camera Operator to roll the film and the Sound Mixer to roll the sound; breaks down the script in terms of its elements (sets, props, stunts, etc.) in order to prepare for film scheduling; prepares the film schedule with input from the Director; determines the number of extras and bits needed for each scene and, with Director's and UPM's approval, hires them.

- <u>2ND ASSISTANT DIRECTOR</u> - often called the Key 2nd; supervises other 2nd Assistant Directors; coordinates their tasks and reports to the 1st AD and to the UPM.

- <u>2ND 2ND ASSISTANT DIRECTOR</u> - generally responsible for supporting all cast; prepares and distributes daily paperwork (call sheets, production reports, actor's time sheets, etc.); assists the Key 2nd in placement of Extras and in maintenance of crowd control; supervises the work of the Directors Guild of America (DGA) Trainee.

- <u>DGA TRAINEE</u> - individual who has passed a rigorous written and oral examination to become enrolled in a 2-year training program, administered by the DGA; assigned to films as additional labor for the Assistant Director team; often used to coordinate extras in large atmosphere scenes; pick up lunches; run errands for the Director; at the end of 2nd year, the trainee becomes a DGA member at the 2nd 2nd AD level.

- <u>SET PRODUCTION ASSISTANT</u> - the PA on the set; reports directly to the 2nd AD.

<u>SCRIPT SUPERVISOR</u> - records detailed notes on every take, including dialogue, gestures, actions, lens used, costumes, makeup, etc. to ensure the continuity of the elements from shot to shot and scene to scene (for example, it would look awfully silly if, during a dramatic scene, the star is wearing glasses, then the camera cuts to a close-up and mysteriously the glasses have disappeared. It is the Script Supervisor's job to make sure that mismatches such as this do not occur); notes are submitted at the end of the day and are used by the Director and Editor when editing the film.

LOCATION MANAGER - scouts for locations for the film, evaluates their suitability, then takes panoramic photographs of the location which are shown to the Director and Production Designer; arranges for permission and negotiates the terms for using the location; organizes all details that relate to that location (permits, parking, catering, police, firemen, etc.).

> • ASSISTANT LOCATION MANAGER - assists the Location Manager, mostly with paperwork, but occasionally by finding locations.

PRODUCTION ACCOUNTANT - responsible for keeping an account of all the money spent while shooting the film; maintains up-to-date accurate financial records of daily costs; reports to the UPM and Line Producer.

> • 1ST ASSISTANT AUDITOR - the Production Accountant's right hand; assists with the preparation of daily and weekly cost reports; supervises the other auditors.

> • 2ND ASSISTANT AUDITOR - assists the 1st Assistant Auditor.

> • PAYROLL CLERK - prepares and issues payroll to crew; reports to the Production Accountant.

COSTUME DESIGNER - conceives and draws designs for the wardrobe worn by the cast, contributing to the overall look of the film and the interpretation of the characters in the film.

- <u>MEN'S LEAD COSTUMER</u> - supervises the construction, fittings, and maintenance of the male actor's wardrobe.

- <u>WOMEN'S LEAD COSTUMER</u> - supervises the construction, fittings, and maintenance of the female actor's wardrobe.

- <u>ON-SET COSTUMER</u> - maintains the costumes on the set or on location.

<u>KEY MAKEUP ARTIST</u> - supervises the application of makeup on the actors; often applies the makeup for the lead actors.

- <u>ADD'L MAKEUP ARTIST</u> - may only apply makeup from the top of the actor's head to the breastbone and tip of fingers to the elbows.

- <u>BODY MAKEUP ARTIST</u> - makeup applied everywhere else on the actor's body is covered by this artist.

<u>PROSTHETIC MAKEUP DESIGNER</u> - designs and supervises the application of latex rubber pieces on an actor's face and head to alter the look of the character; can often include colored contact lenses and false teeth.

<u>KEY HAIR STYLIST</u> - supervises the cutting, coloring, and styling of the hair of the actors and wigs for actors; often performs the styling for the lead actors.

• ADD'L HAIR STYLIST - cuts, colors, and styles the hair of the actors and wigs for actors, usually handles the Bits and Extras while the Key handles the Lead Actors.

DIRECTOR OF PHOTOGRAPHY - (DP, DOP, or Cinematographer) responsible for establishing how the script is translated into visual images based on the Director's requests; decides which camera lenses and film stocks will be used on the

production; maintains the continuity of lighting from scene to scene; works with camera operator to set the composition from shot to shot; sets the camera positions based on the director's request.

• CAMERA OPERATOR - maintains composition as instructed by the Director or DP; watches to make sure the proper eyeline and scene directions are maintained; approves or disapproves each camera take after it is shot; works closely with the 1st Assistant Cameraman (1st AC) during rehearsals and camera takes to assure proper focus, zoom and dolly moves; works closely with the sound department to insure proper placement of microphones; works with 2nd Assistant Cameraman (2nd AC) regarding the proper size and placement of actors' marks indicating their position in front of the camera.

•1ST ASSISTANT CAMERAMAN - (1st AC) duties include changing lenses; keeping the camera in working order; maintaining focus and zooms during shooting; sets up camera at the start of each day; loads and unloads film magazines into the camera; resets the footage counter after each re-load; sets lens T-stops prior to each take at the direction of the DP; measures distances to subjects during rehearsals; checks to make sure no lights are bouncing or glaring into the lens.

- 2ND ASSISTANT CAMERAMAN - (2nd AC) duties include clapping the slate for each shot; keeping camera reports; placing marks for actors; prepares exposed film for delivery to lab; maintains film and expendables inventory; when a Film Loader is unavailable, loads and unloads film magazines without scratching the film stock.

- FILM LOADER - loads & unloads film magazines without scratching the film stock; fills out camera reports; keeps the loading room and camera truck in order.

- STILL PHOTOGRAPHER - takes still photographs on the set to be used for matching continuity in later shots and for publicity purposes.

PRODUCTION DESIGNER - responsible for the physical look of the film; designs all sets and supervises all set decoration; knowledgeable in architecture, design, and construction, etc.

- ART DIRECTOR - responsible for and supervises every aspect of the film's decor and set construction; knowledgeable in architecture, design, construction etc.; reports to the Production Designer.

- SET DESIGNER - plans the construction of the sets from the description and drawings of the Art Director and/or Production Designer; drafts the blueprints for the construction crew.

- ILLUSTRATOR - aids the Production Designer with drawings of the Designer's ideas should the Designer not draw; works closely with the Set Designer.

SET DECORATOR - responsible for dressing the set with furnishings relevant to the scene.

- LEADMAN - 2nd in command to the Set Decorator; supervises the swing gang.

- SWING GANG - responsible for the placement of furnishings on a set, called "dressing the set", and the removal of the furnishings when the set is no longer in use, called "striking the set."

PROPERTY MASTER - (Prop Master) responsible for the maintenance, availability and placement of all hand props on the set.

- ASSISTANT PROPERTY MASTER - assists the Prop Master.

CONSTRUCTION COORDINATOR - supervises the construction crew insuring that the sets are constructed according to the blueprints drawn by the Set Designer.

- CONSTRUCTION FOREMAN - the construction coordinator's right hand; supervises the construction of the sets and the construction crew.

- CARPENTER - often called a Hammer or Prop-maker; constructs the sets according to the blueprints.

- PLASTERER - plasters any areas of the set that require plastering.

- LABORER - responsible for picking up and delivering materials and supplies to the construction crew.

- PAINTER - paints the sets that need painting under the direction of the Art Director.

- STANDBY PAINTER - available on set during photography in case any set pieces needed touching up with paint.

- STANDBY GREENSMAN - responsible for placement of plants and trees on the set; spray paints leaves to match the seasons called for in the scene.

VIDEOTAPE PLAYBACK OPERATOR - organizes and supervises the playback of videotape for on-camera scenes; maintains the "video assist" playback monitor and system for the Director. The video assist monitor is available to the Director so that he can watch on videotape playback the scene that was just photographed to make sure he is happy with the performance and camera movement.

- VIDEO PLAYBACK ASSISTANT - assists the Video Playback Operator.

PRODUCTION SOUND MIXER - responsible for recording the voices of the actors on each take of film.

- BOOM MAN - handles the microphone boom and assists with clip-on, radio, cordless and other types of microphones.

- CABLEMAN MAN - often referred to as the Utility Cableman; handles the sound hook-ups; manages the many cables and wires to protect them from damage.

CHIEF LIGHTING TECHNICIAN (GAFFER) - responsible for lighting on the set according to the instructions of the DP; supervises placement of the lights before and during filming.

- BEST BOY GAFFER - 2nd in command of department; supervises other electricians and the electrical equipment.

- ELECTRICIAN/LAMP OPERATOR - sets and adjusts lighting equipment.

- GENERATOR OPERATOR - turns on and off the generator; maintains it in proper working condition.

KEY GRIP - responsible for the movement of set pieces on location or on the soundstage; supervises the grip crew with the movement of set pieces, some construction pieces, some camera dolly equipment, and occasionally some lighting equipment;

works directly with the Gaffer and DP providing necessary assistance and labor.

- BEST BOY GRIP - 2nd in command of department; supervises other grips and the grip equipment.

- COMPANY GRIP - provides labor on the set for laying dolly tracks, moving set pieces, moving lighting, altering stands, etc.

- DOLLY GRIP - provides labor for moving the camera dolly according to the directions of the DP and Camera Operator; assists in laying the dolly track.

- CRANE GRIP - provides labor for moving the various grip cranes according to the directions of the DP, Camera Operator and Key Grip.

FIRST AID/NURSE - provides competent medical services to cast and crew on location and on stage.

SPECIAL EFFECTS COORDINATOR - (SPFX Coord) designs, organizes and supervises any effect that is special, extraordinary and/or must be created, including rain, mud, fires, explosions, shattering glass, etc.

- SPECIAL EFFECTS FOREMAN - the SPFX Coordinator's right hand; supervises the SPFX crew; assists in the creation of effects.

- SPECIAL EFFECTS STANDBY - assists in the creation of effects.

- WIND MACHINE OPERATOR - turns on and off the wind machine fans; maintains it in proper working condition.

VISUAL EFFECTS SUPERVISOR - coordinates and supervises the optical effects of the film (matte paintings, blue screen, opticals, creature designs, prosthetic designs, miniatures, etc.) and the visual effects crew.

CRAFT SERVICE - responsible for maintaining coffee, beverages and snacks on the set; sweep up, and doing small chores.

CATERER - organizes and prepares meals on location for cast and crew.

TRANSPORTATION COORDINATOR - supervises the drivers and all transportation equipment and vehicles for the film; organizes and coordinates shipping of materials and equipment to and from location.

- TRANSPORTATION CAPTAIN - the Coordinator's right-hand; supervises the Drivers.

- DRIVERS - driving and maintaining all transportation equipment and vehicles.

EDITOR - assembles the film in a defined order (to tell a story) for display on a screen in a movie theater; often entails as much creative input as the Director.

- **1ST ASSISTANT EDITOR** - Editor's right-hand; has an efficient filing and coding system for keeping track of thousands of feet of film; talks with the labs and visual effects companies; relieves Editor of having to do jobs other than editing.

- **2ND ASSISTANT EDITOR** - works with Editor to synchronize the film print soundtrack so that when the film is projected, the sound of the actor's voices coincides with the movement of the actor's mouths; catalogues and keeps dailies organized and accessible; splices film; keeps the Editing Room in order.

- **APPRENTICE EDITOR** - handles miscellaneous tasks for the Editing crew while learning the different responsibilities of Editor and Assistant Editor.

COMPOSER - writes the music for a film score, augmenting and enhancing the visual elements of a film.

UNIT PUBLICIST - responsible for the promotion and publicity of the film through radio, TV, newspapers, magazines, etc.

JOINING THE UNION

Should you reach a point where you feel it is advantageous or maybe necessary to join one of the local craft unions, there are some considerations that you should be aware of.

Getting Into IATSE

The IATSE and Basic Crafts Unions represent the thousands of workers employed in the numerous labor positions on film and television productions. The IATSE and Basic Crafts Unions negotiate with the Alliance of Motion Picture and Television Producers (AMPTP) regarding working conditions, competitive pay rates and health and welfare benefits for their members. Most other major cities such as New York, Chicago, and San Francisco have their own Local Offices for many of these crafts. Pay rates will vary from city to city.

The majority of the film and television production in Los Angeles is done under union contract. However, there is and probably always will be non-union work in LA as well. While some non-union productions provide a competitive wage, the primary difference between union and non-union work is the fact that a non-union employee is not provided with pension, health and welfare benefits. A union member is guaranteed these benefits as part of the Basic Agreement negotiated between the IATSE and Basic Crafts Unions and the AMPTP.

"How do I join the IATSE?" It's the old "Catch 22": you can't become a member of the union until you're employed on a union production, and you can't work on a union production until you are a member of the union. Sounds like it is impossible to get in, right? Well, there are a couple of ways.

"Making Your Days"

The most common way of joining one of the motion picture and television IATSE locals is to "make your days". As part of the by-laws of each Local Office, the union has established a criteria for eligibility into the union. The chief criteria is working a minimum of 30 days as an employee on one non-union production, or 100 days on a multiple of non-union productions in a fiscal year, in a position that is represented by that specific local. Although 30 days is generally the standard, each local may vary, so check with each local for the exact number of days. For example, if a person wishes to join the Cameraman's Union Local 600, he must work a minimum of 30 consecutive or non-consecutive days in the entry-level position of a Film Loader on one production. The employee must be able to prove he has worked in this capacity by providing the following information for each day of work he is claiming as part of his 30 days:

- copy of the applicant's deal memo (it is usually a one-page form detailing the working conditions and pay scale the applicant is given on the production; usually the applicant signs the deal memo the first day he begins employment on a production)

- copy of the I-9 Form with back-up documentation (the I-9 is required by the Immigration & Naturalization Office of the US Government to prove the applicant is an American citizen)

- copies of paychecks or pay stubs

- copies of call sheets and production reports

- copies of staff and crew lists

- copies of any production memorandums prepared by the applicant during production

Once the 30 days have been completed, and copies of the paperwork are prepared in an organized and clear manner, the non-union person can apply to the Local office for membership by submitting all the paperwork to the Local Business Agent, or BA, accompanied by a cover letter asking for membership into the Local. Each Local has a BA who is responsible to his membership, insuring that the membership requirements are being met, membership dues are paid, and the working conditions, labor rates, and fringe benefits are being met according to the Basic Agreement negotiated with the AMPTP.

The BA will review the application and paperwork for accuracy and honesty. Should all of the information prove truthful, the BA will offer the non-union person membership into that Local. The employee must pay his membership initiation fee (which varies from $200-6000 depending upon the particular craft Local) and in return, he is given a membership card and his name is placed on the Industry Experience Roster. This Roster is made available to all film productions intending to employ union members and indicates those IATSE members whose dues have been paid in full and are eligible for employment on union film productions. For a list of the current BAs representing the IATSE Locals in Los Angeles, see the Appendix.

Permits

Every once in a while, the film and TV industry will suddenly become so busy that all of the IATSE members in one particular Local may be employed. Nevertheless, there is still a need for labor on productions which the Local IATSE Office cannot fill. When such an event occurs, the Local Office will "go out to permits." The term means that due to the fact that they cannot supply the labor needed, the Local Office will give permission to a production to allow the employment of non-union labor in positions where union labor would normally be employed. This gives all non-union labor a chance at working on a union production. The days worked will count toward the 30 days membership eligibility requirement.

The BA is one of the individuals who can recommend qualified non-union labor to a Producer when permitting is granted. Needless to say, the BA is someone a non-union laborer should get to know if the non-union laborer wants to join the Local. When permitting occurs, the BA will review his records for the names of individuals he feels are qualified non-union laborers that he can recommend for work. If the non-union laborer's name is in his records, there's a good chance the laborer will be offered employment.

Being offered a chance for employment by the BA creates a potential window of opportunity for entrance into the membership of the Local Office. Once the non-union employee has worked 30 days on one production, or 100 days on multiple productions in one fiscal year, consecutively or non-consecutively, the Local Office will deem the employee eligible for membership into the IATSE. The employee must pay his membership initiation fee and in return, he is given a membership card and his name is placed on the Industry Experience Roster.

Sounds easy, huh? Unfortunately, "going to permits" doesn't happen often. But when it does, be ready!

Another valuable contact who can be influential in a non-union laborer obtaining work when permits are allowed is the Head or Supervisor of Studio Construction. Each Studio has its own head of construction who supervises the construction on its film and television sets. Much like the BA, the Head of Construction can recommend non-union labor when the industry "goes out to permits." If you don't personally know any of these individuals, try contacting a friend who is working as a carpenter, an electrician, or a grip as the case may be, on one of the studio's productions and ask him to introduce you to the head of construction. A list of the current Studio Construction Heads can be found in the Appendix.

When a Non-Union Production is "Organized"

On occasion, a non-union production shooting in Los Angeles is large enough or visible enough to become a target by Local IATSE Offices for organization. Essentially what happens is that a few Union representatives, generally the Local Office BA and a few Local Members, will visit the set of a film or television production shooting in Los Angeles. Without disrupting the daily work, they begin to talk to non-union members about "organizing" the production into a union production. What they are suggesting is that the non-union labor force on the production band together and go "on strike" while asking the Local Office BA to represent them in negotiating working conditions and wages. The hope is that the strike will disrupt the production sufficiently to warrant the Producers of the production to come to an agreement with the BA, resulting in the conversion of the show from a non-union to a union production.

The advantage to non-union employees of the "organization" of a production is that anyone employed on the show at the time of the union negotiations must be offered membership in the union when the show is converted to union status.

I am aware of one person who benefited from such an "organization effort." He was employed on a television show as a 2nd Assistant Cameraman when the show was organized. He had only been working in the film industry for three months when the organizing effort began, and as a result, he became a union member as a 2nd Assistant Cameraman. Instantly, his hourly wage increased from $10/hr to $18/hr. Currently, a union 2nd Assistant Cameraman's hourly wage is $29/hr.

Keep in mind, however, a non-union production is not obligated to negotiate with an "on-strike" non-union labor force. The Producers of the production can decide to hire other non-union labor to replace those individuals who have walked off the job. In that case, tough luck - they're out of their jobs.

The Producers can also invite the "on-strike" non-union labor back to their jobs with better pay rates and over-time provisions, but still not offer fringe benefits.

Both of these situations happen on occasion, but not very often. However, when a non-union production goes on strike in Los Angeles, it becomes very difficult for the Producers to maintain any work force as most laborers, union or not, will not cross a picket-line.

THE MOTION PICTURE STUDIOS

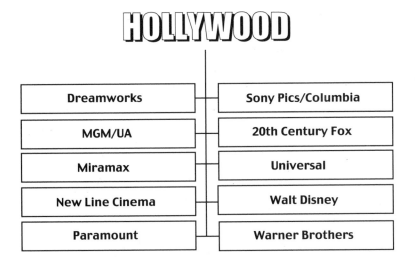

The individuals in the previous sections are not the only people involved in the making of a film. Films are often financed by a major motion picture studio such as Walt Disney Pictures, Warner Brothers Pictures or 20th Century Fox Films. Each studio has its own structure and titles. However, the positions on the next few pages have been standardized to give you an idea of the various types of studio executives behind the camera involved in the making of a film. Almost everyone of these executives have an Assistant.

THE CREATIVE GROUP

PRESIDENT/HEAD OF PRODUCTION - the head of all film production for the studio; has the authority to give the go-ahead to produce a film from one of the studio's screenplays (green-lighting a film); involved in all big producer deals, large literary acquisitions, and star casting.

SR VP, PRODUCTION - most of the same authority as the President, but cannot greenlight a film; oversees the development and production of films, occasionally overseeing a large solo project without intervention from the President (developing a film is the process whereby a studio purchases a screenplay from the writer for a negotiated price, then the studio hires the writer or other writers to write or re-write the screenplay, based on comments and notes from one or more studio executives).

VP, PRODUCTION - oversees the development and production of scripts that he and the Creative Executives have found; often must "pitch" their idea or script to the President or Sr VP to get the go-ahead to develop it.

DIRECTOR OF CREATIVE AFFAIRS - intermediate level between the VP and Creative Executive; usually someone who is on a fast track to a higher position, but not quite ready for VP level; looks for scripts which can be developed and ultimately produced by the studio.

CREATIVE EXECUTIVE - (CE) a junior executive who helps senior executives supervise development and production; reads scripts; writes story notes; generates cast and director lists.

THE PHYSICAL PRODUCTION GROUP

PRESIDENT/PHYSICAL PRODUCTION - the head of all physical production for the studio; has the authority to approve all production budgets when films are greenlit by his creative counterpart, the President/Head of Production; is usually the supervisor of the higher-budgeted, more complex and often sensitive productions.

VP, PHYSICAL PRODUCTION - oversees the physical production of greenlit films (the nuts-and-bolts of making the film); approves the hiring of the line producer & unit production manager; liaison between the production company and the studio's creative executives assigned to the film; trouble-shoots daily production of film.

EXECUTIVE PRODUCTION MANAGER - an experienced DGA UPM hired in a staff position to supervise, negotiate and approve all labor and equipment deals; usually only visits the set if a major problem occurs that the Production Executive cannot handle; also supervises the Production Executive.

PRODUCTION EXECUTIVE - (PE) usually assigned to two or more films at a time; prepares initial production plan for the film (i.e. schedule, budget, locations, key crew recommendations, etc.); also provides recommendations on the structure of the production company (should it be an in-house production, a stand-alone company or subsidiary company?) before the Director, Line Producer and UPM are hired; provides liaison between the filmmakers and the studio; usually visits the set at start of photography, reappears half-way through, then returns at the end to assist wrap-up of production; will visit the set more frequently if production problems arise; needs to be as knowledgeable of studio's requirements as he is about the filmmakers' needs.

THE POST-PRODUCTION GROUP

VP, POST-PRODUCTION - oversees the post-production period of films (editing, mixing, scoring, dubbing, etc.); approves the hiring of the editing team; liaison between the post-production team and the studio's creative executives assigned to the film; trouble-shoots daily post-production of film.

POST-PRODUCTION SUPERVISOR - usually assigned to two or more films at a time; prepares initial post-production plan for the film before the filmmakers are hired, which includes schedule, budget, key crew recommendations, lab deals, etc. ; liaison between the post-production team and the studio; usually visits the post-production offices at start of post-production, then reappears at key deadlines to insure delivery requirements are being met.

THE LEGAL GROUP

VP, LEGAL & BUSINESS AFFAIRS - oversees all legal aspects of films in development and in production; approves the contracts of all ATL and BTL talent; assigns outside counsel when film is designated an Article XX, Negative Pick-Up Deal, or Acquisition; supervises project attorneys.

The designations just mentioned refer to the many ways that a film can be financed by a film studio. *Article XX* refers to the 20th clause of the union agreement between the AMPTP and the IATSE which says that a studio, which is signatory to the IATSE Agreement for the use of union labor, has the right to finance a non-union film as long as it notifies the IATSE 30 days prior to the start of principal photography. This notification period allows the IATSE to try to "organize" the film by convincing the crew hired to work on the film to become members of the IATSE locals. The IATSE can also avoid the hiring of non-union labor by insuring that qualified union labor is available for employment, prior to the start of photography, in the city in which the film will be made.

Negative Pick-Up refers to a studio or independent financier agreeing, before shooting of the film begins, to purchase or "pick-up" the negatives of the exposed film from the production company for a pre-negotiated fee. With such an agreement, the studio is merely "funding" the film and not "producing" it. This allows the production company to use non-union labor in an effort to keep costs low, a method a studio could not utilize because of its union agreement. The down-side for a studio with such an agreement is that as a financier and not a producer, the studio cannot exert any creative control over the film. Any attempts at creative influence over the production can be construed by the unions as "functioning in a producer capacity" which is in violation of the union/studio agreement.

Acquisition refers to buying the exposed negative of the film from a Producer once the Producer has completed photography of the film but has not gone into post-production including editing. By acquiring the film at this stage of film production, the studio or independent financier can now exert creative control over post-production, marketing and the eventual release of the film. With this, and many more ways, of producing a film, you can see why a studio must employ a skilled legal team.

PROJECT ATTORNEYS - assigned to one or more films at a time; prepare and negotiate ATL & BTL talent contracts; negotiate all union/labor agreements; supervise, negotiate and approve all location contracts and music clearance deals.

THE FINANCE GROUP

VP, PRODUCTION FINANCE - supervises the budgeting, estimating and daily/weekly cost reporting of films in development and production; assists in setting up the structure and bank accounts of outside companies when it is determined that the film will be produced as an Article XX, Production/Finance Deal, Negative Pick-Up Deal, or Acquisition; negotiates and locks-in exchange rates for foreign productions; has initial approval over all film budgets.

DIR, PRODUCTION FINANCE - 2nd in command and has most of the same authority as the VP, Production Finance; often visits set when financial problems arise or cost reports reflect questionable figures, or the danger of an over-run.

SENIOR AUDITOR - assigned to one or more pictures at a time; tracks daily costs of production and reports to the studio executives; approves daily and weekly cost reports; often visits set at least once for EFC Meeting (Estimated Final Cost).

MGR, BUDGETING & ESTIMATING - works with the Production Executive (PE) in developing a budget for film before it is greenlit; supervises and organizes budgets from various studio departments; assists Director and Producer in preparing their budget for submission to the President for approval and greenlight; maintains lists of current studio labor and equipment rates; investigates rates and working conditions of competitive films; publishes variety of budget vs. actual cost analyses.

ANCILLARY GROUP

<u>VP, PRODUCTION RESOURCES</u> - supervises the acquisition and trade-out agreements for the placement of products prominently displayed in a film (i.e., Campbell Soup in a kitchen, Sony stereo in an office, etc.); assists Producer with negotiating cast and crew accommodations on location, often obtaining significant discounts.

<u>DIR, PRODUCTION RESOURCES</u> - assists the VP with negotiating the trade-out and acquisition of products for placement in film; assists Producer with negotiating cast and crew accommodations on location, often obtaining significant discounts; tracks on a daily basis delivery deadlines of all products and their placement in films, insuring that the product is given the exposure required per the product agreement with the filmmakers.

SELECTING A CAREER TRACK

Now that we have reviewed the positions behind the camera, you need to decide which career track to follow. As you can see by these positions, there are essentially two "areas" in which one can pursue a film career - the creative group or the production group.

The creative group covers every aspect of getting a film ready for production including story development, talent representation, deal-making and ultimately, creatively producing a motion picture. Most major producers, agents and studio executives have emerged from a career in the creative group because, more often than not, the deal is more important to getting a film produced than are the crafts involved in actual production.

The production group trains people in the skills involved in the physical production of making a film. People on a production path learn about every aspect of physical production from set construction to sound mixing. If you want to be a DP, Editor, UPM or Line Producer, or even a Director, then the production group is probably for you.

I began my career as an actor and director in the theater with a college degree in Theater and practical experience in the New York theatrical community. When I moved to Los Angeles to continue my career, I could not find work because my background was not in film and television. Knowing that one day I wanted to produce and direct motion pictures, and yet knowing very little about how to make a film, I realized I had to leave the creative side and enter the production side in order to educate myself in the process of filmmaking.

Over the last ten years, my career history looked something like the chart in Figure 13. This is only one example of a career path. Both the creative and production groups encompass hundreds of separate career paths. What you need to do is figure out which group is for you and, ultimately, to which ca-

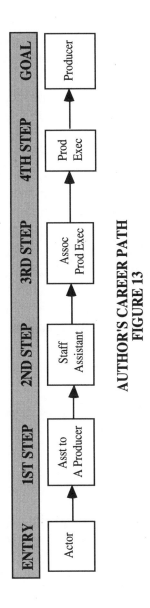

AUTHOR'S CAREER PATH
FIGURE 13

reer goal do you aspire? Once that decision is made, you can then develop a game plan for yourself. Based on the final goal, what is the entry level position for that group? Remember, you can always change your mind and your career track.

Let's examine a few possible production choices. Take a look at Figure 14. As you can see, there is no one unique way to attain your career goal. You can, however, help yourself focus on your goal by establishing your career path in advance. Now let's take a look at a few possible creative choices as illustrated in Figure 15. When developing your own career path, if you know the goal you seek, but aren't sure of the best entry level position in which to start, ask others who have attained certain goals for their advice. Be warned, however, no two people will give you the same answer - everyone gets there in their own way. Finally, look at Figure 16 which illustrates career paths in the technical areas of filmmaking. Keep in mind that all of these charts show possible avenues for a career. It doesn't mean that these are the only routes to success or that they are available when you are ready for them.

COVER LETTERS

Cover letters have been and always will be a controversial subject. The cover letter can either get you in the door for an interview, or turn the reader off and end up in the trash. So, how do you know what to say?

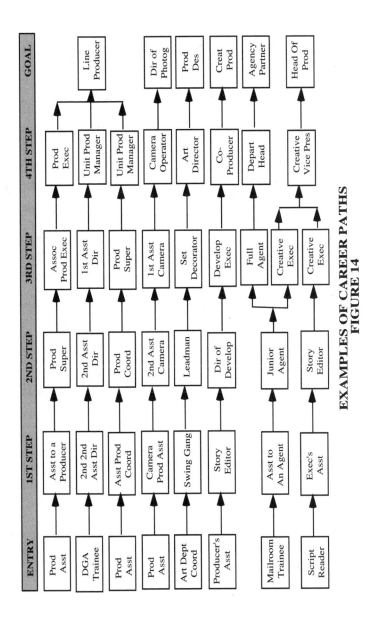

EXAMPLES OF CAREER PATHS
FIGURE 14

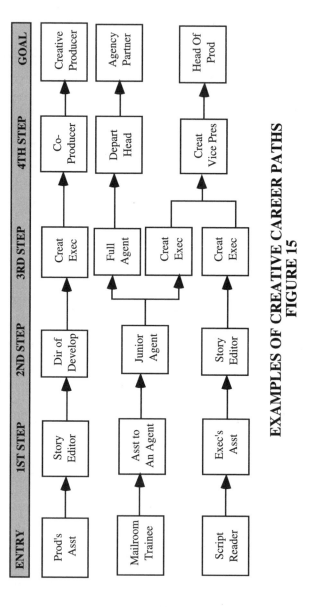

EXAMPLES OF CREATIVE CAREER PATHS
FIGURE 15

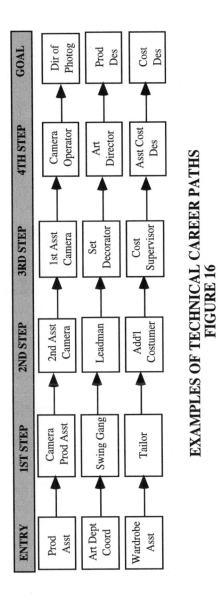

EXAMPLES OF TECHNICAL CAREER PATHS
FIGURE 16

There are two types of cover letters: informational inter-view letters and employment-seeking letters. Don't confuse one with the other, that's almost as bad as lying on your resume. The informational interview letter is a one page letter in which you ask someone for an interview for the purpose of gaining advice on how to get started in the industry.

This letter is straight-forward and to the point without being pushy, arrogant or presumptuous. Keep the letter to three paragraphs, four maximum. Check your spelling - if someone sends me a letter with even one misspelled word, it says to me that the individual either doesn't know how to spell or doesn't take enough pride in his work to insure that it's the best it can be. Either way, it goes right into the trash. If the letter works and you are offered an interview, *DO NOT ASK FOR A JOB OR A JOB LEAD.* This would be working under a false pretense since your letter indicated you only sought advice. If a job lead comes up in the conversation, let it be at the invitation of the host or hostess, not from you. An example of this type of letter can be found in Figure 17.

The other type of cover letter is one that seeks employ-ment. You can use this type of letter to respond to an advertise-ment for a position, to follow up with someone you've met who may be able to offer employment opportunities, or to introduce yourself to an individual at a production company where you'd like to work, even if they have no idea who you are. My first mailing of resumes was done with this type of letter. Rather than just sending a letter blindly, I tried to find something out about the individual I was writing to as a lead-in or introduction.

With this letter, you indicate from the start that you are in LA to pursue a film career. However, don't fall into the trap into which most people just starting out fall: asking for work

John Doe
100 Anywhere Street
Los Angeles, CA 90068

August 31, 1998

Mr. Bigtime Producer
Star Entertainment
1000 Lankershim Blvd.
North Hollywood, CA 91604

Dear Mr. Producer,

I am writing to seek your advice on the subject of careers in feature film
production. I feel that with your experience, you might be able to offer
advice to a newcomer like myself on how to get started in the industry.

I am a recent graduate of Carnegie Mellon University in Pittsburgh, PA
with a degree in Drama. In the last year, I wrote and directed a stage play
which has been nominated for a Ford Foundation Grant in playwriting.
Since my ultimate goal is to be a writer-director, the creative area appears
to be the best place to start.

Please understand that I am not asking for a job, nor am I asking for leads
to any job openings. On the contrary, I am seeking your advice on how to
begin working towards my goal.

I understand that you are a busy man. If it is at all possible, I would like to
arrange a brief informational interview. I will call your office next week to
see if a time can be scheduled. I have enclosed my resume and references
for your perusal.

Sincerely,

John Doe

INFORMATIONAL INTERVIEW COVER LETTER

FIGURE 17

because they want to learn. No one will hire you because *you* want to learn. They *expect* you to learn. ***They will hire you be-cause you can provide a service they need***. By indicating your skills and experience, you are showing what services you can provide. If the services sound interesting to the recipient, and he is looking for someone to fill that need, chances are you'll get an interview.

This letter should also be no longer than one page and no more than three to four paragraphs. Use good grammar and check your spelling. Don't be too familiar with the person, even if you've met them once before. Always be professional. Don't write your letter in pen and ink, use a typewriter or word processing program. If you're doing a mass-mailing, try not to let your letter look like a form letter. An example of this type of letter can be found in Figure 18.

THE FOLLOW-UP

After sending out your letter and resume to the prospective interviewer, wait 1-2 weeks before contacting his office. Have a pen and paper with you when you make the call so you can make notes from the conversation. When you call, chances are you won't get the person you wrote to on the phone, but rather his assistant or secretary. Be polite and courteous to this person. The secretary is your meal-ticket to the boss. Keep detailed records of your conversation: when you called, who you spoke to, if and when they told you to call again, advice or guidance they offered, someone else they referred you to, etc. Your first phone call may go something like this:

HER: Good morning, Bigtime Producer's office. May I help you?

YOU: Good morning. This is John Doe. I mailed my resume to Mr. Producer about a week ago and I am calling as a follow-up to obtain an inter-

John Doe
100 Anywhere Street
Los Angeles, CA 90068

August 31, 1998

Mr. Bigtime Producer
Star Entertainment
1000 Lankershim Blvd.
North Hollywood, CA 91604

Dear Mr. Producer,

I am a graduate of the Drama Department of Carnegie Mellon
University in Pittsburgh, PA with a degree in Writing. I have
moved to Los Angeles to pursue a career in motion pictures.

At Carnegie Mellon, I wrote and directed a stage play which
has been nominated for a Ford Foundation grant in playwriting.
I also produced and stage managed the 1997 New Play Festival
comprised of 15 new plays performed in repertory, while
directing two of the plays. It is with these skills and experience
that I feel confident that I can provide you with solid script development supervision.

I have enclosed my resume for your perusal. I understand that
you have a busy schedule. If it is at all possible, I would like to
arrange an interview. I will call your office next week to see if
a time can be scheduled.

Sincerely,

John Doe

AN EMPLOYMENT-SEEKING COVER LETTER

FIGURE 18

YOU: Thank you. Do you mind if I call back in a couple of weeks?

HER: Sure.

YOU: Terrific. Thanks very much. Oh, by the way, what is your name?

HER: Deena.

YOU: Great. Thanks for your help, Deena.

Now, you know it's going to be tough to get the interview, but you also found out the assistant's name. Over the next day or two, drop the assistant a note thanking her for taking the time to speak with you, and that you'll contact her again in a couple of weeks. Then make a note on your calendar to call her in two weeks. Next time, you place the call *to her,* not to the boss. Try and get her to respond to you more conversationally, more informally. Try and turn her into your ally. If you succeed in getting her on your side, sooner or later she'll get you in to see the boss.

Create an index card file of all the people to whom you send resumes and the sequence of follow-up calls you make. This way, when someone calls you back, you have a quick, easy reference of the history of communication with that individual's office.

THE INTERVIEW

When you get the interview, you will want to work very hard to be prepared before you walk into the interviewer's office. Find out as much as you can about the person you are meeting with and/or his company. You can learn this information by regularly reading the trade papers (*The Hollywood Reporter & Daily Variety*). If the individual or company has been involved with any films, rent those movies if they're on videotape and watch them. You can also look up their names in reference books at the library, or on the Internet Movie Database located at www.imdb.com, or at one of the industry bookstores which are listed in the Appendix.

Look professional at your interview. Men in coat and tie, women in dresses or business suits. Be yourself. Don't try and be someone you're not. Don't feel you have to know all the answers. It's better to say you don't know than to offer an answer that is obviously made up to mask your ignorance.

Don't be afraid to ask questions, but make them intelligent questions. Find out in advance of the interview as much as you can about what he does, how he got to where he is, where he's going in the future, what advice can he offer, etc. An active, inquisitive mind is much more appealing than a stagnant, bored mind.

If you're visiting on the basis of an informal information session, have a list of questions you want to ask and be straight forward about the questions. In other words, ask your questions with conviction, don't make your comments in a half-hearted, intimidated way. Your host will be much more impressed with you if he senses confidence. And follow up his comments so as to establish a dialogue, a repartee, rather than a simple question and answer session. Don't just sit and nod your head at the answer you hear. Build on what you've just heard and carry on that subject until you feel it's right to move on to the next question.

Visits for the purpose of seeking employment are much trickier. While you want to present a positive, confident, knowledgeable image of yourself, you also don't want to come across as negative, arrogant, and a know-it-all. In my book, humility goes a long way. Be yourself. Speak in a clear and concise manner with enthusiasm and interest. The interviewer will build on some of the things you say by offering leading questions. Pick up on them. Don't try to skirt an issue because you have something else about which you want to talk. He has obviously found it important enough to ask about it, so take the time to answer the question, then move on to another area which you think may be of interest to him.

Present your resume if he does not have one handy. Remember, the resume is a brief description of who you are - the interview is your opportunity to expand in greater detail on some of the points in that resume. Recognize that this interview is not just an opportunity for your host to find out about you, but also a chance for you to find out more about him. So, take the time to find out more about him or the company. It may help you decide whether or not you'll want to work for him or the company if a job is offered to you.

Don't overstay your welcome. If you get a sense that the meeting is wrapping up, even if it's shorter than you had anticipated or wanted, get yourself up and get out of there. The interviewer will appreciate the fact that you know when to leave (it's also a strong sign of professionalism). Thank him for his time on your way out. If you've been in an employment interview, try to get a sense of whether or not it would be appropriate to call again in a week or two to follow up on any job opportunities, but don't push the issue if you sense that it's inappropriate. And finally, don't forget to thank the assistant on the way out (today's assistant may become tomorrow's studio chief!).

When you get home after your interview, before you do anything else, write down on an index card your thoughts about the interview, the person you met, the company, when you should follow up with a call (add this note to your calendar as well), whether or not it's a person or company for whom you'd want to work, who you can get to call the interviewer on your behalf as a reference, etc. If you don't do it now while it's fresh in your mind, you'll forget about it the next day and you'll have lost some valuable information.

Then, draft two thank you letters: one to the interviewer and one to his assistant who helped you in setting up the interview. Don't mail them immediately. Wait one or two days, take a second look at the letters and see if there is anything in the letter you should change (tone, familiarity, etc.), then type up fresh copies of the letters and mail them.

WHERE TO LOOK FOR WORK

Now that you know how to go about preparing yourself and your resume for work, how do you know who to contact for a job? There are a number of resources you can turn to that will give you this information. The names and addresses of these resources are listed in the Appendix, but for now, let's look at a couple of them.

The Trade Papers are always a good source for job leads. *The Hollywood Reporter* and *Daily Variety* are the two primary trade magazines. Both daily papers can be purchased at your local newsstand and at some bookstores for $1.00. A one-year subscription to The Hollywood Reporter is $155.00 and a one-year subscription to Daily Variety is $157.00. You won't always find the leads for jobs in the Help Wanted listings. Sometimes you need to "read between the lines" of the articles in the trades.

For example, if you're seeking a creative job in a studio, then you may have noticed that Joe Smith has been given greater responsibilities, supervising both film *and* television production for The Motion Picture Production Company. Why not write him a letter, congratulating him on his new position, commenting that under his guidance you believe the company will do well, and the fact that you'd like to be a part of that team. The article in the trades didn't indicate that any jobs were available at this company, but maybe if you send a sharp cover letter and your resume, Mr. Smith will be intrigued and offer you an interview. Or he may pass it on to one of his VPs of Production and ask him to interview you. Either way, you've created an opportunity for yourself. That's why it pays to read the trade papers daily.

If you're looking for work on a film in a crew position, the trade papers also have listings once a week indicating all of the films in production world-wide, and all of the television shows in production in North America. Feature film listings appear on Tuesdays and television productions appear on Thursdays. Documented in the trade papers will be the name of the show, the key crew attached to the project (Director, Producer, UPM, etc.), the film locations, the scheduled shooting dates, a mailing address, and a phone number. Try mailing your resume to the Producer or UPM on each production and tell them you are available for Production Assistant work. Then follow up your mailing with a phone call three to five days later.

Another source for similar types of listings is the *Backstage West/Dramalogue*. A weekly paper which comes out on Thursdays, *Backstage West/Dramalogue* lists a number of union and non-union feature films, graduate student films, student films, commercials, industrials, etc. which are looking to hire crew. It is available at newsstands, bookstores and 7-Eleven stores for $2 per issue, or you can purchase a one-year subscription for $65.

Another fine source is the *Hollywood Creative Directory* (HCD). HCD is updated every four months, and lists every major studio, major production company, and most minor production companies in both film and television. A typical listing in the HCD looks like this:

DEAD END PRODUCTIONS
PHONE:...818-555-1000
FAX:... 818-555-1110
01 Dead End Street, Suite 45
Studio City, CA 91604

TYPE: Motion Pictures + Television
CREDITS: The Incredible Story

Richard Wannabee..President
Peter Y. Iduno...VP, Production
Susan Sellsalot..Dir, Creative Affairs
Michael Pitchtome...Creative Executive

The listing tells you the name, address, phone and fax numbers of the company, what type of projects they do (MP-motion pictures, TV-television), whether or not they have a development deal with another company, the titles of some of the projects they have been involved with in the past, and who the executives and/or decision makers of the company are. HCD is available for $49.50 for a single issue, or as a one-year subscription, updated three times a year for $120. Call them for more information, or to place an order, call 800-815-0503 outside California, or 310-315-4815 in California. You can also e-mail them at hcd@HollyVision.com. You might ask your local librarian if they have a current copy of any of these resources, or if they can obtain one for the library for you to use.

You can also look for free-lance film crew jobs on the callboards of the USC and UCLA Film Schools. Students enrolled in these film schools always need additional crew to help in the making of their student films. Many successful director, producers, agents, etc. have come from these two training programs. And you never know when the student director you're helping with his student film will become the next Ron Howard.

THE ACTOR

"I'M GONNA MAKE YOU A STAR!"

"You're likely to earn your first money as an actor about one year after the day you get your SAG card."

- a SAG actor overheard at a party

"An actor, especially an unemployed one, is the greatest salesman alive. And the product for sale is the salesman."

- a former agent, now a studio executive, overheard at a lunch meeting

As I've said earlier, you've spent the last four years working on craft and technique, focusing on your art. You now must shift gears and begin focusing on your business. Just as the Ford

Motor Company has a product for sale called a Ford Explorer, there exists a company called the Joe Actor Company and its product for sale is you - an actor. The keys to the success of selling you, the product, are first, having the right tools with which to prepare the product for sale, and second, the marketing of the product.

TWO KEY ITEMS: HEADSHOTS & AUDITIONS

In the section entitled THE BASICS earlier in this book, we discussed the important tools a beginner needs to start a career in the film industry. Those items included a resume, an appointment book, an answering machine, etc. Very quickly, let's review the key items that **should be** found on an actor's resume:

- Your Name - no nick-names, unless you use a nick name professionally.

- Agency Name - if you have an agent, go ahead and list his name and telephone number.

- Your Phone Number - while you may list your home number, it is probably better to list a service number or pager number to protect yourself from being bothered at home by unwanted phone calls.

- Union Affiliations - if you are a member of any of the 4A's, you should definitely indicate this.

- <u>Height, Weight, Hair Color, Eye Color</u> - this is necessary for actors.

- <u>Film and TV Credits</u> - if you have any.

- <u>Stage Credits</u> - if you have any.

- <u>Special Skills</u> - if you have any.

- <u>Training & Education</u> - list your collegiate information here. It often helps to indicate the names of selected instructors that may be recognizable to the entertainment industry - it may spark some interest in the reader if he is familiar with someone who instructed you.

Display this information in an easy-to-read and organized fashion. An example of a good generic actor's resume is illustrated in Figure 19.

And now here's what **should not** be on the resume.

- <u>Age</u> - in this industry, you can often be considered "too young" or "too old." Better to keep them guessing. Actors should also refrain from listing their age range as it can limit you and keep you from being seen.

- <u>Dates</u> - again, keep them guessing and don't limit yourself.

JANE DOE

| Height | 5'7" | Hair: | Honey | | AEA/SAG/AFTRA |
| Weight | 118 | Eyes: | Blue | | The Bigshot Agency • 818-555-1212 |

FILM

Paying the Price	Co-Star	Disney
Brewster's Millions	Featured	Director: Walter Hill
Harold's Dilemma	Star	USC Grad Film

TELEVISION

Beverly Hills 90210	Co-Star	Fox
Life Goes On	Co-Star	Warner Brothers
Summer Fantasies	Featured	Orion Productions
C.O.N.D.O.R.	Featured	Orion Productions
Network Nerds	Star	Group W. Cable
Clouds	Star	Century Cable

STAGE

Girl on the Rocks With a Twist	Marilyn	Angels Theater
People in the Wind	Cherie	Angels Theater
Firing Chamber	Della	Coast Playhouse
Crimes of the Heart	Meg	South Bay Perf. Arts Center
Reluctant Saint	Angelina	En Scene
Clouds	Susie	En Scene
Oliver	Nancy	MBCC Presents
Southern Exposure	Julip	The Powerhouse Stage
Midsummer Night's Dream	Hippolyta/Cobwebb	Whitefire Stage
Guys & Dolls	Adelaide	Skylight Dinner Theater
Picnic	Madge	Actors Alley Theater

VIDEO/INDUSTRIAL

Tom McDonald	Lead	TRW
Clean Air	Lead	GTE
Cost Care	Lead	Lyon Recording
Interview Techniques	Lead	Medcom
Music Video/Sergio Mendez	Lead	Page 2 Productions
Your Mental Health	Lead	Robinson Productions
TRW - (10)	Lead	TRW
Ralphs Grocery Co.	Lead	Ralphs Grocery Co.

COMMERCIALS
Available on request

WORKSHOPS/CLASSES

Danny Simon	Comedy, Writing
Brian Reise	Cold Reading
Joan Darling	Scene Study
Adam Roarke	Film Technique
Lou Diamond Phillips	Film Technique
Mark Malis	Cold Reading Mastery
Tepper/Gallegos	Commercial Acting Workshop
David Beaird	Scene Study &
	Advanced Technique

INTERESTS
Member - "Company Of Angels" Theater Company
Member - "Artifical Intelligenz" Improv Group

EXAMPLE OF AN ACTOR'S RESUME

FIGURE 19

- <u>Social Security Number, Home Address, and Home Phone Number </u>- it is too easy to find out personal and financial information about you and your family by listing this information. It is no one's business but your own. You can provide your Social Security number to your employer when you are given the job.

- <u>Community Theater Credits</u> - "Community" isn't the best of words; so try to emphasize the character or quality of the work: instead of saying "Watertown Community Music Theater", say "Watertown Music Theater". At this stage in the game, no one need know such minor details that suggest an "amateur!"

- <u>The word "Resume"</u> - using this word at the top of your resume may insult the reader's intelligence.

- <u>Measurements</u> - again, keep them guessing. You don't want to give any information that can potentially "seduce" the wrong people.

- <u>Emphasis on Singing and Dancing</u> - in Hollywood, people tend to think Singer and Dancers can't act.

- <u>Nothing cute or autobiographical</u> - be professional!

Cut your resume to fit your headshot. Since your headshot is usually 8" by 10", and standard bond paper is 8 1/2" by 11." you need to trim your resume paper to fit the headshot size. It looks cleaner and more professional this way. More about headshots in a moment.

I want to repeat an important note about resumes: *DON'T LIE!* Film professionals will check your credits. Some of them may know individuals on some of the shows in which you are supposed to have appeared. All they need to do is make a call and BANG! There goes the job prospects and a very good contact down the drain, as well as your reputation.

Now let's look at the next two most important tools for an actor: the headshot and the interview/audition.

The Headshot

A headshot is an 8" x 10" photograph of your head and shoulders from which a Casting Director, Producer or Director can tell what you look like. Lately, it has become more accepted as well as popular to have your headshot actually be a three-quarter body shot, capturing your image from head to knees. Either format is acceptable. However, you'll need to shoot new pictures every three years or so, or when you make a dramatic change to your appearance (cutting off shoulder-length hair to very short hair, for example). If you change agents, often they will ask that you shoot new headshots as well.

Your headshot should capture your special quality. It should be a perfect example of who you are deep inside. Don't airbrush the scars and wrinkles away - it makes you look too perfect and no one is perfect. Casting Directors want to know that the picture they see is exactly what will walk through their door for an interview. If it's not, they generally are annoyed enough to never call you back again. An example of a good headshot is illustrated in Figure 20.

Tamara Zook

EXAMPLE OF AN ACTOR'S HEADSHOT

FIGURE 20

There are two types of headshots: Commercial & Theatrical. The Commercial headshot looks like you've just come straight out of a musical. It should have a big smile, show lots of teeth, be happy, warm, and perky. The Theatrical headshot is more serious, dramatic, striking. It indicates your "type" as an actor.

How do you know what your "type" is? Ask yourself these questions:

- how am I normally cast?

- what have my friends told me about my acting personality?

- is there any known star or actor I am often compared to?

- what roles on TV/film/stage could I do without stretching?

The answers to these questions will help tell you your type. Some examples are Young Leading Man, Young Leading Lady, Character Male, Character Female, Comedian, Comedienne, etc. These are the industry standard "actor types" that appear in the Academy Players Directory, about which I will say more later.

Finding A Photographer

If you don't have a headshot, you need to get one done. So, how do you find a photographer? Well, you're bound to meet other actors shortly after arriving in town. Try asking them if you may see their headshots. Look at their photographs and see if you like the work. Check the trade magazines as many of them publish advertisements placed by photographers. Once you think you've found a photographer whose work you like, check up on him before committing to him. Getting the photographer's answers to the following questions will help you in determining if he is the right photographer for you:

How do you handle a photo session?

- if his plan is to sit you down and start shooting you without saying anything, chances are your pictures will reflect an uncomfortable subject. If, instead, he begins talking to you, guiding you, making suggestions on how you should hold your head, or comment on an expression you make that the camera seems to like, etc., your photos may be much more real.

How much do you charge?

- the going rate these days for a headshot session is anywhere between $175-500.

How many rolls of film will you shoot?

- it varies, but a good photographer will shoot anywhere from 2 to 4 rolls of film, 36 exposures on each roll.

How many costume changes will you allow?

- generally that's up to you. However if a photographer says you only get one look, you should find another photographer. It makes sense to try different outfits as each piece of clothing says something unique and different about you.

Who will handle my makeup: me or your makeup artist?

- if he has a makeup artist, I'd talk with that person to find out what type of makeup she uses and how much makeup he plans to use on you. If you're uncertain about the person, ask the photographer if you can do your own makeup. The last thing you want to have happen is for your pictures to come out with you looking like a clown from Ringling Brothers Circus!

How long will it take until I get my proof sheets?

- it should be a relatively quick turn-around, say around two weeks. If it's going to take longer than that, find out why.

How many prints from my session are included in the price and how long will it take until I get the prints?

- this is negotiable, but usually you'll get four or five. It should take the photographer no more than three weeks to turn them around to you.

Who keeps the negatives from the shoot?

- usually the photographer does, but if you can get the negative, it will save you the cost of having to make an inner-negative from one of your prints when you go to a photo lab to have large quantities of your prints made (an inner-negative is a negative made by taking a photograph of one of your prints).

What happens if I don't like my proofs?

- this is a very important question to ask. The fair an- swer is that the photographer will photograph you again in a new session, creating the same amount of exposures as he did the first time, without charging you a penny. It's fair to ask a photographer to do this once if you're unhappy with the results, but it's abusive if you ask him to do it more than once.

Can you recommend a good but inexpensive photo lab who can mass-produce my prints?

- if you're new in town, you won't know where to go to have this done, so it's not a bad idea to ask his opinion. But keep in mind, the photographer may get kick-backs for every person he sends to the lab. Make sure you check out other labs as well as the one he recommends.

Planning the Shoot

You've made a decision on a photographer. The next thing to do is decide what look you wish to have. Do you want a Commercial or Theatrical shot, or both? If you're shooting a Commercial photo, wear medium to light-colored clothing: it helps set up a happier, warmer mood. For a Theatrical photo you can wear darker clothes to bring out the drama in you. Either way, stay away from wearing black, white, loud plaids, prints, shiny fabric, and jewelry. Bring lots of clothes to your photo session and get the photographer's opinion on what to wear. His experience with this sort of thing can be extremely valuable.

The Proofs

Once you've finished the shoot, and you have a proof sheet, you need to pick those shots from the proof sheet which represent you the best. Those shots are the ones from which you want prints made. Don't pick the shots yourself. It's tough to be objective about yourself. Get other people's opinions. Ask your photographer for his opinion. If anyone can tell what's best for you, he can. Ask your agent for his input, other actors, anyone who is film-wise. But don't ask your boyfriend or girlfriend, your mother or other relative. *They* always think you look great. Their input won't be appropriate for this type of photograph.

The Prints - the Pre-Printing Decisions

You've chosen the shots to be printed, now there are a few decisions to be made about what type of prints you want. Here are your choices:

- Glossy: it looks shiny, it's the most often used and least expensive way to go

- Matte: provides a cloth-like look and feel

- Gloss-tone: a toned-down version of the Glossy, similar to what you would see in magazines

- Borders: the white space between the photograph and the edge of the paper it's printed on. You should keep borders narrow, about 3/8".

- Bleeding: the photograph fills up the paper all the way to the edges

- Knock-Out Name: a small block of white space with your name printed in black lettering within the block

- <u>Overlay Name</u>: no white space around your name, essentially the name appears directly on the photo in black letters

- <u>Reverse Overlay</u>: same as above only with white letters

The choice of print type is a very personal one. It is totally up to you on what you want your final print to look like. However, the one golden rule is to make sure your name is located somewhere on the front of your print, even though your resume is attached to the back of the print. It would be a catastrophe for your picture and resume to end up on the desk of Robert Zemeckis and somehow the resume be separated from the picture and it become lost. Zemeckis looks down at your picture, thinking to himself that he has found his star for *Forrest Gump II*. But when he turns over the picture and finds no resume, he throws your photograph in the trash. Why? Because there was no name on the photograph and he didn't want to spend his valuable time trying to figure out who the heck you are!

Choosing a Printer

Next, you need to choose someone to do the printing for you. Use the same mechanism for finding a printer as you did the photographer. Ask other actors you have met in town who they have do their printing and set up an appointment to meet them. When all else fails, check the *Yellow Pages Phone Book* for a listing of photography developers and set up an appointment to meet them.

Keep in mind that the cheapest printer is not always the best printer. While you don't want to have to spend an arm and a leg for prints, you do want the work to be of good quality. Choose the company you want to use by asking them these key questions:

What will the Inner-negative cost ?

- if you were unable to secure the negative of your print from your photographer, you'll need to have an inner-negative made. This is a negative created by taking a photograph of one of the prints. From the inner-negative, more prints are made. Generally, an inner-negative should cost about $10-15.

What will the prints cost ?

- prints made in bulk are usually cheaper, so I'd recommend ordering 200-300 prints for starters. An average cost for 100 prints is approximately $60.

What do the "extras" cost ?

- as I've said before, it's strictly a personal choice on how you want your headshot to look. But to give you an idea of cost, I've listed an average price for most of the frequently used "extras:"

    - cropping - $3/set-up

    - bleeding - $15/neg., $0.90/print for 50

    - overlays - $12/first neg., $7.50/add'l use

• lighten/darken areas of photo - negotiable

Academy Players Directory

This "smart investment" book is published every 4 months by the Academy of Motion Pictures Arts and Sciences (the people that bring you The Oscars). For actors, it is the next best thing to having an agent. It consists of four volumes of photographs of actors.

To appear in the Directory, you must be a member of a union or represented by a franchised agent. Then all you need to do is pay the fee and your headshot can appear in it. The categories you may be listed in are Young Leading Man and Young Leading Lady, Leading Man and Leading Lady, Character Men and Character Women, and finally, Comedians and Comediennes. You may choose the category in which you would like to be listed. You can appear in more than one category, all of them if you like. It costs $75 per category to be listed in the directory.

If you think it's a lousy gimmick, think again. Even top actors like Tom Cruise still appear in the books. You never know when a Casting Director, Producer or Director will be searching the book for the actor with that special look. If you're in there and he sees you, he just may contact your agent to call you in for an audition.

An important note: although you may have chosen to use a three-quarter headshot, be aware that the Academy Players Directory will not publish three-quarter photographs, only headshots.

GENERAL INTERVIEWS

Even though you've done your homework, prepared your scenes, and are ready to audition, chances are you'll only be asked to a general interview by the Casting Director. Don't be disappointed. A general interview can lead directly to work. The purpose of a general interview is to introduce your look, type, voice and personality to the Casting Director. There is, however, work you can do to prepare yourself for the interview:

- Be Interesting. In other words, have a sense of humor. At the same time, don't think you need to be Robin Williams. If you're naturally quiet, then be quietly interesting. Just remember not to clam up.

- Be Interested. Talk to the person. If the Casting Director starts to talk about the new car he bought, then follow it up by asking about how he made the decision to go with that car, or how the car does on mileage.

- Control the Interview. Even though the Casting Director controls the questions, you control the answers, so make the answers mean something.

- Be Yourself. Don't try to be something you're not. Stop worrying about what *is* you and just *be* you. Be clean and neat. There is no dress code for a general interview. Nevertheless, don't wear provocative clothing, it's a turn-off. And lay low on the jewelry.

- <u>Always Bring a Resume and Headshot</u>. It's good to have one just in case they can't find the one they already have of you. But only offer it to the Casting Director if he asks for one.

- <u>Don't Be Late</u>. Give yourself plenty of time to get lost and plenty of time to get ready once you've arrived.

Some of the questions a Casting Director asks can be anticipated. You might want to practice coming up with answers for them so you're not caught off guard. Try your answers out on another actor or a friend to get a sense if it's sounding natural and intelligent. Here are a few of the questions usually asked with which you can practice:

- <u>Tell Me About Yourself</u> - this means be interesting, tell them what interests you. Don't start reeling off credits or they'll reel you out the door. The Casting Director wants to see what personality lies underneath that cover.

- <u>What Have You Done Recently?</u> - pick 1 or 2 of your best credits and find something interesting to say about them. The Casting Director doesn't need to know that the credits you're speaking of may not necessarily be your most recent credits.

- <u>How Old Are You?</u> - answer it, then drop it. Age can limit you. And don't reply with the cutesy answer, "How old do you want me to be?" This will only annoy the Casting Director.

- <u>What Brought You To LA?</u> - "This is where the business is" might be a good answer, not "My boy friend lives here."

- <u>Do You Have an Agent?</u> - yes or no, as may be the case, but if you're not thrilled with your agent, don't start bashing him in this interview. He may be best friends with the Casting Director.

- <u>Do You Have Anything On Tape?</u> - again, yes or no, as may be the case. If you have tapes, bring them with you. But if not, don't feel you need to apologize. You'll eventually have a lot on tape.

- <u>Can You Do a Skill?</u> (juggling, dialects, etc.) - say yes only if you actually can do the skill. In the case of dialects, don't reply using the dialect. It's too cutesy!

Above all, in your general interview, keep these thoughts in mind:

- Be yourself. Be natural, comfortable and spontaneous.

- Don't be negative

- Don't be hostile (no matter how bad your day is going)

- Don't talk in a vacuum. Listen to what the interviewer says and respond to it.

- Don't try to be Robin Williams. There's a difference between having a sense of humor and having an act.

- Know when to leave.

Cold Readings

If the Casting Director asks you to do a cold reading, you know your General Interview has gone exceptionally well. A Cold Reading is auditioning with a script in hand, usually receiving the script shortly before the audition and performing "cold." It's a make-or-break deal. Read well, you may get the job. Read poorly and it may be tougher to get back in for any other audition.

During a cold reading, a Casting Director is looking for three things:

- when you walk in to the reading, what kind of feeling does the Casting Director "get" from you?

- what kind of feeling does the Casting Director "get" from you as an actor during the reading?

- does the Casting Director like you as a person?

Cold reading is not an art, it's a skill that can be learned and learned well. Keep in mind you don't have a lot of time with your preparation so you must make decisions fast. Because of this, no one expects a full-blown performance.

Here's how a cold reading works. Scripts are usually available 24 hours in advance. Try and dress to suggest the part. Be at least 30 minutes early so that you can ask questions about the script from the Casting Director or Casting Coordinator. Don't be afraid to ask, they're there to help.

Get your eyes out of the script, they are the key to your "expression behind the person." Casting Directors want to see your eyes. Focus your eyes on the person with whom you are reading. If you have to look down at the script to pick up a line, fine. Once you've got the line, bring your eyes back to the person with whom you are reading. At the same time, don't memorize your part. If anything, memorize your first and last line so you can start and end with eye contact.

Ignore all stage directions. Do what comes naturally with your movement. Don't use props, they'll only get in the way. Don't get cute by changing the motivations of the character to make things interesting. Just play what's written. Don't create a "character," play yourself. Casting Directors are looking for naturalness. Don't talk yourself into believing you're not right for the part. The Casting Director wouldn't have called you in if he didn't think you were right. Don't overwork the scene. Spontaneity is everything. Don't be afraid to be nervous. Nervousness will get your energy up.

If you're called in to read and you're not ready, ask the Casting Director for more time. Don't ever read if you're not ready. Then again, don't take all day preparing. If you have the entire script, read the whole script, not just the scene. It'll help you better understand the story and characters. Say your lines out loud. The first time you hear it, it won't sound right. By the time you're called for the reading, you'll have "heard" the lines sounding right.

Pick a direction and go with it: how does the character feel and what does he want? Don't worry about being wrong. Practice going out on a limb with your choices. If you flub a line, start over. No one will mind. You are almost always given a second direction after reading, so don't let it throw you. They just want to see how quickly you can change and take direction. If you're asked to read a different scene or character, ask for time to prepare.

COMMERCIAL AGENTS

In the earlier section entitled "The Basics," I discussed the importance of agencies and representation to a beginning film professional. Actors, though, are in a unique position in the film and television industry in that they can often be represented by two types of agents: the Theatrical Agent and the Commercial Agent. Theatrical Agents represent actors for feature film work as well as episodic and sitcom television work. Commercial Agents represent actors strictly for the lucrative business of television commercials.

Commercial agent relationships are different than theatrical agent relationships. While theatrical agent relationships are more one-to-one with smaller client loads, it's not uncommon for a commercial agent to represent a hundred or more clients. Because so many commercials are produced every year, this means that there are more opportunities for actors to be cast.

Naturally, then, commercial agents can afford to take on many actors at once.

Bigger agencies are generally more trusted by casting directors when it comes to commercial work. The easiest way to get representation from one of these agencies is to send them a really, really terrific headshot. A few of the bigger agencies, listed alphabetically, that you may wish to contact are:

> Abrams-Rubaloff & Lawrence
> Nina Blanchard
> Cunningham, Escott & Dipene Agency
> Joseph, Helfond & Rix
> Tyler Kjar Agency
> Sutton, Barth & Vennari

The easiest way to get representation from one of these agencies is to send a really, really terrific headshot.

What You and The Commercial Agent Can Expect of Each Other

A relationship with a commercial agent is different than that with a theatrical agent. Here's what the commercial agent will expect of you:

- **NOT** to get your own commercials

- **NOT** to call with suggestions on submissions

- keep his office stocked with pictures and resumes

- be on time and don't miss interviews

- pay him his commission

- be reachable

- keep track of your residuals and conflicts. Residuals are the monies you receive each time the commercial airs. National commercials make a lot more money than local commercials. If you do a Goodyear Tire commercial, it would be considered to be a "conflict" to do a Michelin Tire commercial. Usually your contract won't allow it.

And what can you expect of your commercial agent? Very simply, he should get you out on commercial calls far more often than you are sent out for films or television; i.e., at least twice a week.

THE ACTOR'S CATCH-22

This is a "film town". Actors generally seek to join SAG and AFTRA first before they join Equity, AGMA or AGVA. But there are stumbling blocks that appear as you seek membership. The "Catch-22" is this: you cannot audition for a SAG film until you have your SAG membership card, and you cannot get your SAG membership card until you have been offered work on a SAG film. So how do you get past this predicament?

Getting into SAG

There are a few ways to get into SAG. The following "tricks to the trade" are essentially the same for all of the performer's unions, but for the moment, we will focus only on SAG, AFTRA and Equity:

- Taft-Hartley - you're a non-union actor, but you audition for a Producer who casts you in his union film. To do this, he makes you sign a Taft/Hartley agreement. The term "Taft-Hartley" refers to the names of two United States Senators who authored the labor law that carries their name (Robert Taft, one of the two Senators, lost to Dwight D. Eisenhower for the Republican nomination for President of the United States in 1952). The Taft-Hartley law is viewed as extremely anti-union by the unions. This agreement allows you to work in a union film as a non-union performer, then work up to 30 days in other non-union films before you must join the union. If you are offered another union role within those 30 days however, you must then join SAG to perform that role. It gets a little tricky because a Producer must prove to SAG why he hired you over a union member. Otherwise, abuses could occur. For example, a Producer might cast an actor in the role of an "Auto Mechanic" and notify SAG that the actor was actually an automobile mechanic, making him the most logical choice for the role over the other SAG actors the Producer auditioned. The automobile repair expertise of the actor might have been minimal at best, but the Producer was a friend of the actor and did the actor a favor. Needless to say, if the Producer is caught lying, he opens himself to a potential lawsuit.

• Unscripted Line - while working as a non-union Extra on a union film, the Director gives you a line to speak that is not in the original script. Immediately, the production company is required to "upgrade" you to a SAG "Day Player" Contract and you become eligible to join the union.

• Extra Work - by working any combination of 3 days as a SAG Extra, you are eligible to join the Union. However, if you think getting a SAG job is tough, try getting a SAG extra job!

• Join AFTRA - be hired to perform an AFTRA role and one year from that hire date, you may join SAG. How do you get into AFTRA? It's simple: go down to the AFTRA office today and buy your membership. It is actually that easy.

• Be hired to perform an Equity role and one year from that hire date, you can join SAG.

• Be hired to perform an AGVA role (singers, magicians, clowns, stand-up comics, nightclub & circus performers, etc.) and one year from that hire date, you can join SAG.

• Be hired to perform an AGMA role (classical singers, dancers, soloists, choral singers, opera singers, etc.) and one year from that hire date, you can join SAG.

Getting Into Equity

There are also ways to get your Equity card:

- A Producer hires you as an actor or stage manager on a union stage production, then you are eligible to join Equity.

- Be hired to perform an AFTRA role and one year from that hire date, you can join Equity.

- Be hired to perform a SAG role and one year from that hire date, you can join Equity.

- Enroll in the Equity Membership Candidate Program. By working 50 weeks over any length of time at any number of Equity Theaters as either an actor, understudy or stage manager, you can become eligible to join Equity.

A FINAL WORD

Well, a couple of hundred pages or so later and you're on your way. You've just had a short introduction to beginning your working career in the film industry. A great deal of information has just been run past you, probably more than you can quickly absorb. But, to summarize the "meat and potatoes" of the book, consider these ten points:

- Plan Your Move to LA. If you've decided that it's time to move to Los Angeles, plan your trip and arrival *before* you get in the car. Think about what you will need to survive in Hollywood and act accordingly.

- Invest In Your Career. If you aren't serious about your career, no one else will be. Equip yourself with quality tools and use them to best represent you, e.g., if taking a class at Panavision will help you be better prepared as a director, then take the class.

- Always Be Professional. No matter where you go, no matter who you meet, always act professionally. Show up on time to meetings, dress appropriately, and do your homework before you arrive at meetings. If friends and colleagues act unprofessionally, don't associate with them.

- <u>Never Stop Networking.</u> This industry is like no other; it is built on contacts. The more people you know, the more skilled you are at telephoning people you don't know, the greater your employment opportunities. Never stop networking.

- <u>Get Into A Coaching Group.</u> Meet regularly with five or more individuals like yourself who are seeking employment. Discuss each other's goals. Be accountable for each other's success while building a larger network for future goals.

- <u>Never Stop Learning.</u> Take classes in screenwriting and editing for a better understanding of these two crafts. Polish your writing skills through creative criticism that can be found in writers' workshops. If you're an actor, don't stop taking classes in acting, movement, speech, voice, improvisation, etc. Don't be afraid to ask colleagues and mentors questions. Maintain your thirst for knowledge.

- <u>Assess Your Career.</u> Be willing to take a hard look at where you are as you progress, and act accordingly. Don't be afraid to make a change in your career within the industry. I started out as an actor, but now I work as a studio executive!

- <u>Keep Up With Changes In the Industry.</u> Stay on the cutting edge. Be conversant with the new technologies such as computer generated imagery, electronic editing, motion capture techniques, etc. The more conversant you are with new technologies, the more the opportunities will occur.

- Never Lie. The fastest way to end a promising career is by not telling the truth. Being imaginative is okay. Even a little embellishing can be acceptable. *But never lie.* You're only as good as your word.

- Never Give Up. If you believe that you can do anything, others will, too. Never give up. Keep a positive outlook at all times. Set mini-goals for yourself that are attainable on a weekly or bi-weekly basis. It will help strengthen your confidence and keep your long-term goal within reach.

This book is intended to shorten both the path and the time needed to start your film career. Much of what I've written about comes from my own experiences and mistakes. If you take the advice I've given, *your* mistakes will be minimal and *your* successes will be bountiful.

Should you need assistance, guidance, or advice along the way, I am available for personal coaching by telephone or in person, group coaching in person, and seminars, all for a very nominal fee. You may contact me for coaching sessions in one of the following three ways:

U.S.A. Mail:	Philip Nemy c/o Angel's Touch Productions 22906 Calabash Street Woodland Hills, CA 91364 USA
E-Mail:	captainnemo2@earthlink.net
Fax Machine:	818-222-2389

APPENDIX

COSTS • EXPENSES • PRICES

EXPENSES FOR YOUR FIRST WEEK IN LA

Apartment Rent (average: 1st mo., last mo., security)	$1,500.00
Telephone (installation & first bill)	70.00
Utilities (installation & first bill - gas, water, electricity)	240.00
Answering Machine	100.00
Groceries	100.00
Total	**$2,010.00**

EXPENSES FOR FIRST SET OF TOOLS

8 X 10 Headshot session	$200.00
8 X 10 Heashot printing (500 theatrical, 500 commercial)	500.00
Resumes (typing and printing 500)	100.00
Typewriter	200.00
Postage (500 mailings @$.33 each)	165.00
Regular Manila Envelopes	50.00
Mailing Labels	35.00
Set of Stationary (about 250 sheets)	75.00
Thank You Notes	25.00
Appointment Book	20.00
Index Card File & Notebook	20.00
One Year Listing in the Academy Players Directory	75.00
SAG Agency List (free to SAG members)	0.25
Resource Directories	200.00
Total	**$1,665.25**

EXPENSES AS YOU BEGIN TO GET WORK

SAG initiation fee	$932.00
AFTRA initiation fee	800.00
Equity initiation fee	800.00
Union dues for two unions	165.00
Attending theater performances (10 shows)	100.00
Performing in Showcases (5 shows)	500.00
Acting classes (6 months)	1,200.00
Trade subscriptions (Daily Variety)	157.00
"Now Appearing" Postcards	250.00
Videocassette (includes air-check, stock, editing)	150.00
Total	**$5,054.00**

ITEMS THAT WOULD BE GREAT TO HAVE BUT AREN'T NECESSARY TO SURVIVE

Computer (includes keyboard & monitor)	$1,000.00
Printer	250.00
VCR	180.00
Camcorder	400.00
Beeper	120.00
Passport	65.00
Total	**$ 2,015.00**

PHONE NUMBERS

ACTING TEACHERS
Roy London   818-760-0845
Nina Foch   310-553-5805
Terence Hines   818-760-4808
Kate McGregor Stewart   213-939-3384
Jeff Corey   310-456-3319
Milton Katselas   310-855-1556
Tracy Roberts   310-271-2730
M.K. Lewis   310-826-8118

ANSWERING SERVICES
A Better Connection   323-462-2200
Actorfone West   323-462-6565
Nationwide Paging   800-USA-BEEP
Pacific Bell Message Center   800-427-7715
Sky Tel   800-SKY-PAGE

FILM STUDIOS/COMPANIES
Castle Rock Entertainment   310-285-2300
Columbia Pictures   310-244-4000
Columbia TriStar Television   310-202-1234
Dreamworks SKG   818-733-7000
Hollywood Pictures   818-560-1000
MGM/UA   310-449-3000
Miramax Films   323-951-4200
New Line Cinema   310-854-5811
Orion Pictures   310-282-0550
Paramount Pictures   323-965-5000
Sony Pictures Entertainment   310-244-4000
Touchstone Pictures   818-560-1000
20th Century Fox Films   310-369-1000

20te Century Fox - Family Films	310-369-1000
20th Century Fox - Fox 2000 Films	310-369-2041
20th Century Fox - Searchlight Pictures	310-369-4402
Universal Pictures	818-777-1000
Viacom Productions	310-234-5000
Walt Disney Pictures	818-560-1000
Warner Brothers	818-954-6000

TELEVISION BROADCAST COMPANIES

ABC Entertainment	310-557-7777
CBS Entertainment	323-852-2345
Disney Channel	818-569-7500
Fox Brodcasting Company	310-369-1000
HBO Original Programmming	310-201-9300
Lifetime Television	310-556-7500
MTV Networks	310-752-8000
NBC Entertainment	818-840-4444
Showtime Networks	310-234-5200
Turner Network Television	310-551-6300
United Paramount Network	310-575-7000
USA Network	212-408-9100
Warner Network Television	818-954-6000

GUILDS & UNIONS

DGA	Directors Guild of America	310-289-2000
SAG	Screen Actors Guild	323-465-4600
WGAw	Writers Guild of America West	323-951-4000
AEA	Actors' Equity Association	323-462-2334
AFTRA	American Federation. of Television & Radio Artists	323-461-8111
AGMA	American Guild of Musical Artists	212-265-3687
AGVA	American Guild of Variety Artists	818-508-9984
IATSE	International Alliance of Theatrical Stage Employees	818-905-8999

MAJOR TALENT AGENCIES
Agency for the Performing Arts	(APA)	310-273-0744
Creative Artists Agency	(CAA)	310-288-4545
The Gersh Agency	(Gersh)	310-274-6611
Endeavor	(End)	310-248-2000
International Creative Management	(ICM)	310-550-4000
United Talent Agency	(UTA)	310-273-6700
The William Morris Agency	(WMA)	310-274-7451

STUDIO HEADS OF CONSTRUCTION
Tony Aveta	Walt Disney Television	818-560-1441
Earl Cappello	Sony Studios	310-280-8000
Mike Ivy	Paramount Studios	323-965-5000
Tim James	Universal Studios	818-777-1000
Norm Jost	20th Century Fox Studios	310-277-2211
Pat Whalen	Warner Brothers Studios	818-954-6000

HEADSHOT PHOTOGRAPHERS
Doreen Stone	323-876-2636
Photo Realism/Evan MacKenzie	323-663-0642
Studio B-3/Sunny Bak	310-652-9403
Sandy Spear	323-934-9728
Michael Helms	818-899-8002
Tama Rothschild	323-658-7862

PHOTO LABS & REPRODUCTIONS
Duplicate Photo Labs	323-466-7544
Mike Field	310-220-3082
Producers & Quantity Photo Inc.	323-462-1334
Final Print/Joycelyn Law	323-466-0566
	323-466-5404

MISCELLANEOUS CONTACTS
| Academy Players Directory | 310-247-3058 |
| AFTRA/SAG Credit Union | 800-354-3728 |

Airport Transportation Information	310-646-5252
American Film Institute	323-856-7600
Backstage West/Dramalogue	323-464-5079
Breakdown Services Inc.	310-276-9166
Buses (RTD - LA)	310-273-0910
Buses (RTD - LA)	818-781-5890
Daily Variety	323-857-6600
Department of Motor Vehicles (DMV)	323-461-6257
Department of Motor Vehicles (DMV)	323-744-2004
Department of Motor Vehicles (DMV)	818-901-0550
Department of Water & Power (DWP)	323-481-5411
Equity Hot-line	323-462-0955
Flash Forward	818-558-1890
Hollywood Creative Directory	310-315-4815
The Hollywood Reporter	323-525-2000
Hollywood Reporter Blu-Book	323-525-2000
Independent Feature Project West	310-475-4379
Larry Edmunds Bookshop	323-463-3273
Los Angeles Times	323-237-5000
Pacific Coast Studio Directory	805-242-2722
Panavision	818-881-1702
Resume Service/Michael Barak	310-854-0443
Samuel French Bookshop (Hollywood)	323-876-0570
Samuel French Bookshop (Valley)	818-762-0535
SAG Agency Information	323-856-6821
SAG Film Society	323-856-6655
SAG Hot-line	323-461-1023
Southern California Gas Company	310-839-0525
Southern California Gas Company	323-461-6611
Southern California Gas Company	818-343-3808
Univ. of California at Los Angeles (UCLA)	310-825-4321
Univ. of Southern California (USC)	323-740-2311
Women In Film	323-463-6040
YMCA (Glendale Branch)	818-240-4230

UNION OFFICES

AEA (Stage Actors)   323-462-2334
Business Agent - Michael Van Duzer
6430 Sunset Blvd., Suite 700
Los Angeles, CA 90028

AFTRA (TV & Radio Actors)   323-461-8111
Business Agent - Mark Farber
6922 Hollywood Blvd.
Hollywood, CA 90028

AGMA (Musical Artists)   212-265-3687
Business Agent - There isn't one
1727 Broadway
New York, NY 10019-5214

AGVA (Variety Artists)   818-508-9984
Business Agent - Lon Huber
4741 Laurel Canyon Blvd., #208
North Hollywood, CA 91607

DGA (Directors)   310-289-2000
Business Agent - Susan Hendricks
7920 Sunset Blvd.
Hollywood, CA 90046

SAG (Film Actors)   323-465-4600
Business Agent - Ken Orsatti
5757 Wilshire Blvd.
Los Angeles, CA 90036

WGAw (Writers)   310-550-1000
Business Agent - Doreen Braverman
8955 Beverly Blvd.
Los Angeles, CA 90048

IATSE International   212-730-1770
Business Agent - Mike Proscia
1515 Boradway, Suite 601
New York, New York 10036

IATSE (Stage Employees - Crew)   818-505-8999
Business Agent - Harry Floyd
13949 Ventura Blvd., Suite 300
Sherman Oaks, CA 91423

IBEW 40 (Electricians)   323-877-1171
Business Agent - Tim Dixon
5643 Vineland Avenue
North Hollywood, CA 91601

Local 44 (Propmakers)   818-769-2500
(Greens, SPFX, Drapery, Set Decorating)
Business Agent - Ron Cunningham
11500 Burbank Blvd.
North Hollywood, CA 91601

Local 80 (Grips)   323-931-1419
Business Agent - Jim Buck
6926 Melrose Avenue
Hollywood, CA 90038

Local 600 (Photographers)   323-876-0160
Business Agent - George Spiro Dibie
7715 Sunset Blvd., Suite 300
Hollywood, CA 90046

Local 695 (Sound Mixers)   818-985-9204
Business Agent - David Kimball   323-877-1052
5439 Cahuenga Blvd.
North Hollywood, CA 91601

Local 705 (Costumers)   323-851-0220
Business Agent - Sandy Berke-Jordan
1427 N. LaBrea Avenue
Hollywood, CA 90028

Local 706 (Makeup & Hair)   323-877-2776
Business Agent - Howard J. Smit   818-984-1700
11519 Chandler Blvd.
North Hollywood, CA 91601

Local 724 (Laborers)   323-938-6277
Business Agent - Earl Brendlinger
6700 Melrose Avenue
Hollywood, CA 90038

Local 876 (Art Directors)   818-762-9995
Business Agent - Scott Ross
11365 Ventura Blvd., Suite 315
Studio City, CA 91604

Local 884 (Teachers)   323-650-3792
Business Agent - Paula Bussinger
P.O. Box 461-467
Los Angeles, CA 90046

Local 892 (Costume Designers)   818-905-1557
Business Agent - Carol Frazier
13949 Ventura Blvd., Suite 309
Sherman Oaks, CA 91403

Teamsters Local 399 (Drivers)   818-985-7374
Business Agent - Tony Cousimano
4747 Vineland, Suite E
North Hollywood, CA 91603

Local 727 (Crafts Services)   818-891-0717
Business Agent - Pamela Mack
14629 Nordhoff Street
Panorama City, CA 91402

Local 728 (Gaffer & Best Boy)   818-891-0728
Business Agent - Dean Bray
14629 Nordhoff Street
Panorama City, CA 91402

Local 729 (Painters)   323-877-0671
Business Agent - Carmine A. Palazzo   818-984-3000
11365 Ventura Blvd., Suite 202
Studio City, CA 91604

Local 755 (Plasterers)   818-379-9711
Business Agent - Mark Seay
13949 Ventura Blvd., Suite 305
Sherman Oaks, CA 91423

Local 767 (First Aid)   818-760-5341
Business Agent - Dean Bray
14629 Nordhoff Street
Panorama City, CA 91402

Local 776 (Film Editors)   323-876-4770
Business Agent - Mike Breddan
7715 Sunset Blvd., Suite 100
Hollywood, CA 90046

Local 816 (Scenic Artists)   818-906-7822
Business Agent - Ted Rubin
13949 Ventura Blvd., Suite 308
Sherman Oaks, CA 91423

Local 847 (Set Designers)   818-784-6555
Business Agent - Marjo Bernay
13949 Ventura Blvd., Suite 301
Sherman Oaks, CA 91423

Local 871 (Script Supervisors)   818-782-7063
Business Agent - Roy Gardner
7061-B Hayvenhurst Avenue
Van Nuys, CA 91406

COMPUTER SOFTWARE

Database Software
Filemaker Pro   • for Windows & Mac

Hypercard   • for Mac

Q&A   • for Windows

Dynodex   • for Mac

Film Scheduling Software
Movie Magic Scheduling   • for Windows & Mac

Turbo Ad   • for Windows

Toolkit Film Scheduling   • for Windows & Mac

Film Budgeting Software
Movie Magic Budgeting   • for Windows & Mac

Turbo Budget   • for Windows

Toolkit Film Budgeting   • for Windows & Mac

Script Writing Software
Scriptor   • for Windows & Mac

Screenwriter   • for Windows

Scriptware   • for Windows

Final Draft   • for Windows & Mac

Story Development Software

Dramatica Pro   • for Windows & Mac

Storyline   • for Windows

Collaborator Ii   • for Mac

Storyboard Software

Storyboard Quick   • for Mac

Word Processing Software

Microsoft Word   • for Windows & Mac

Word Perfect   • for Windows

Spreadsheet Software

Microsoft Excel   • for Windows & Mac

Lotus 1-2-3   • for Windows

Graphics Management Software

Microsoft Works   • for Windows & Mac

MacDraw II   • for Mac

Internet Providers

America On-Line   • features film newsgroups
                            where you can post or browse
                            through movie-related mes-
                            sages

Prodigy   • provides box office statistics
                            and the wit and wisdom of
                            critic Leonard Maltin

Compuserve   • features critic Roger Ebert's
                                movie reviews & Magill's
                                Survey of Cinema, a database
                                of articles and films since 1902

Earthlink   • fastest growing provider today

<u>All Software Available At:</u>
Writer's Computer Store   310-479-7774
11317 Santa Monica Blvd.
Los Angeles, CA 90024

MAJOR U.S. FILM FESTIVALS

American Film Institute Festival
P.O. Box 27999
Los Angeles, CA 90027
213-856-7600
213-462-4049 Fax
• Formats Accepted: 35mm, 16mm, and preview on cassette
• Entry Fee - none
• Submission Deadline - Mid January
• Festival Held - Mid June
• Contact - Ken Wlaschin

Aspen Film Festival
P.O. Box 8910
Aspen, CO 81612
303-925-6882
303-925-9534 Fax
• Formats Accepted: 35mm, 16mm, and preview on cassette
• Entry Fee - none
• Submission Deadline - Early August
• Festival Held - Late September
• Contact - Ellen Kohner, Festival Dir.

Chicago Int'l Film & Video Festival
415 North Dearborn Street
Chicago, IL 60610-9990
312-644-3400
312-644-0784 Fax
• Formats Accepted: 35mm, 16mm, 3/4", 1/2"
• Entry Fee: none
• Submission Deadline: Early August
• Festival Held: Late September
• Contact: Ellen Kohner, Festival Dir.

Houston Int'l Film & Video Festival
P.O. Box 56566
Houston, TX 77256
713-965-9955
312-644-0784 Fax
• Formats Accepted: 35mm, 16mm, 3/4", 1/2", Super 8mm (on videotape)
• Entry Fee: $50-200
• Submission Deadline: Early March
• Festival Held: Late April
• Contact: J. Hunter Todd, Festival Dir.

Independent Feature Film Market
132 West 21st Street, 6th Floor
New York, NY 10011
212-243-7777
212-243-3882 Fax
• Formats Accepted: 35mm, 16mm, and preview on cassette
• Entry Fee: $250-400
• Submission Deadline: Mid July
• Festival Held: Early September
• Contact: Ray Schaub, Market Dir.

New York Film Festival
Film Society of Lincoln Center
70 Lincoln Center Plaza
New York, NY 10023-6595
212-875-5610
212-875-5636 Fax
• Formats Accepted: 35mm, 16mm, and preview on cassette
• Entry Fee: none
• Submission Deadline: Early July
• Festival Held: Late September
• Contact: Marian Masone

Palm Springs Int'l Film Festival
401 South Pavilion Way
P.O. Box 1786
Palm Springs, CA 92263
619-322-2930
619-320-9834 Fax
• Formats Accepted: 35mm, 16mm, and preview on cassette
• Entry Fee: none
• Submission Deadline: Early November
• Festival Held: Early January
• Contact: Denis Pregnolato

San Francisco Int'l Film Festival
1560 Fillmore Street
San Francisco, CA 94115
415-567-4641
415-921-5032 Fax
• Formats Accepted: 70mm, 35mm, 16mm, Super 8mm, 3/4", 1/2"
• Entry Fee: none
• Submission Deadline: Early December
• Festival Held: Late April
• Contact: Peter Scarlet, Festival Dir.

Santa Barbara Int'l Film Festival
1216 State Street, Suite 201
Santa Barbara, CA 93101
805-963-0023
805-965-0557 Fax
• Formats Accepted: 35mm, 16mm, and preview on 1/2" cassette
• Entry Fee: $25
• Submission Deadline: Late December
• Festival Held: Late March
• Contact: Phyllis de Picciotto

Seattle Int'l Film Festival
Egyptian Theater
801 E. Pine Street
Seattle, WA 98122
206-324-9996
206-324-9998 Fax
• Formats Accepted: 35mm, 16mm, and preview on cassette
• Entry Fee: $50 features, $10 shorts
• Submission Deadline: Late March
• Festival Held: Mid May
• Contact: Darryl Macdonald, Festival Dir.

Student Academy Awards
Academy of Motion Picture Arts & Sciences
8949 Wilshire Blvd.
Beverly Hills, CA 90211-1972
310-247-3000
310-859-9351 Fax
• Formats Accepted: 35mm, 16mm
• Entry Fee: none
• Submission Deadline: Early April
• Festival Held: Early June
• Contact: Regional Coordinator

Sundance Film Festival
427 Main Street
Park City, UT 80460
801-645-7280
801-575-5175 Fax
• Formats Accepted: 35mm, 16mm, preview on 3/4" or 1/2"
• Entry Fee: $35 features, $10 shorts
• Submission Deadline: Early November
• Festival Held: Late January
• Contact: Nicole Guillemet

Telluride Film Festival
National Film Preserve
Box 1156
Hanover, NH 03755
603-643-1255
603-643-5938 Fax
• Formats Accepted: 35mm, 16mm, and preview on cassette
• Entry Fee: $35
• Submission Deadline: Mid August
• Festival Held: Early September
• Contact: Bill & Stella Pence, Co-Dirs.

USA Film Festival
2917 Swiss Avenue
Dallas, TX 75204
214-821-6300
214-821-6364 Fax
• Formats Accepted: 35mm, 16mm, 3/4", 1/2, beta
• Entry Fee: $35
• Submission Deadline: Early March
• Festival Held: Late April
• Contact: Richard Peterson, Artistic Dir.

BOOKSTORES

Samuel French Theater & Film   323-876-0570
7623 Sunset Blvd.   800-7-ACT NOW
Hollywood, CA 90046

Samuel French Theater & Film   818-762-0535
11963 Ventura Blvd.   800-7-ACT NOW
Studio City, CA 91604

Larry Edmunds Cinema & Theater   323-463-3273
6644 Hollywood Blvd.
Hollywood, CA 90028

NEWSTANDS

Sherman Oaks Newsstand   818-995-0632
14500 Ventura Blvd.
Sherman Oaks, CA 91403

Universal News   323-467-3850
1655 N. Las Palmas Ave.
Hollywood, CA 90028

World Book and News   323-465-4352
1652 Cahuenga Blvd.
Hollywood, CA 90028

TRADE PAPERS

Daily Variety   323-857-6600
5700 Wilshire Blvd., Suite 120
Los Angeles, CA 90036

Backstage West/Dramalogue   323-464-5079
1456 N. Gordon St.
Los Angeles, CA 90028
Mailing Address: P.O. Box 38771
Los Angeles, CA 90028-0771

The Hollywood Reporter   323-525-2000
6715 Sunset Blvd.
Los Angeles, CA 90028

RECOMMENDED READING

"Adventures in the Screen Trade"
    By William Goldman
    Simon & Schuster

"AIVF Guide to Int'l Film & Video Festivals"
    By Kathryn Bowser
    Foundation for Independent Video and Film, Inc.

"Cinematography: A Guide For Film Makers and Film Teachers"
    By J. Kris Malkiewicz, assisted by Robert E. Rogers
    Van Nostrand Reinhold Company

"Dealmaking in the Film & TV Industry"
    By Mark Litwak
    Silman-James Press

"The Devil's Candy"
    By Julie Salamon
    Houghton Mifflin Company

"Film & Video Marketing"
    By Michael Wiese
    Focal Press

"Film Lighting"
    By J. Kris Malkiewicz,
    assisted by Barbara J. Groboski
    Prentice Hall Press

"Film Scheduling"
        By Ralph S. Singleton
        Lone Eagle Publishing

" The Filmmaker's Dictionary"
        By Ralph S. Singleton
        Lone Eagle Publishing

"Final Cut"
        By Steven Bach
        William Morrow & Co.

"How To Sell Your Idea To Hollywood"
        By Robert Kosberg with Mim Eichler
        Harper Perrenial

"Independent Feature Film Production"
        By Gregory Goodell
        St. Martin's Press

"The Independent Film & Videomakers Guide"
        By Michael Wiese
        Focal Press

"Making a Good Script Great"
        By Linda Seger
        Samuel French Publishing

"Making Movies"
        By Sidney Lumet
        Alfred A. Knopf

"Producing, Financing, & Distributing Film"
        By Paul A. Baumgarten, Donald C. Faber
        & Mark Fleischer
        Limelight Editions

"Screenplay" The Foundations of Screenwriting"
        By Syd Field
        Dell Publishing

"The Screenwriter's Workbook"
        By Syd Field
        Dell Publishing

"When the Shooting Stops...the Cutting Begins"
        By Ralph Rosenblum and Robert Karen
        Hyperion Publishing

"Your Film Acting Career"
        By M.K. Lewis & Rosemary R. Lewis
        Gorham House Publishing

EQUIPMENT VENDORS

GRIP EQUIPMENT

Castex Rentals   323-462-1468
1044 N. Cole Ave.
Hollywood, CA 90038

Chapman/Leonard   323-877-5309
12950 Raymer Street
North Hollywood, CA 91605

Cinelease, Inc.   818-841-8282
2020 N. Lincoln St.
Burbank, CA 91504

Concept Lighting, Inc.   818-767-1122
11274 Goss Street
Sun Valley, CA 91352

Grip City   818-994-6508
15338 Oxnard Street
Van Nuys, CA 91411

Hollywood Rental Co., Inc.   818-768-8018
7848 N. San Fernando Rd.
Sun Valley, CA 91352

Leonetti Company   323-469-2987
9420 Chivers Street
Sun Valley, CA 91352

Mole-Richardson Co.   323-851-0111
937 N. Sycamore
Hollywood, CA 90038

Paladin Cine Rentals   323-851-8222
7356 Santa Monica Blvd.
Los Angeles, CA 90046

Paskal Lighting   323-466-5233
6820 Romaine Street
Hollywood, CA 90038

TM Motion Picture Equipment Rentals 818-764-7479
7365 Greenbush Avenue
North Hollywood, CA 91605

LIGHTING EQUIPMENT
Arriflex Corporation   818-841-7070
600 N. Victory Blvd.
Burbank, CA 91502

Castex Rentals   323-462-1468
1044 N. Cole Avenue
Hollywood, CA 90038

Cinelease, Inc.   818-841-8282
2020 N. Lincoln Street
Burbank, CA 91504

Hollywood Rental Co., Inc.   818-768-8018
7848 N. San Fernando Rd.
Sun Valley, CA 91352

Kino Flo, Inc.   818-767-6528
10848 Cantara Street
Sun Valley, CA 91352

Leonetti Company   818-252-1900
9420 Chivers Street
Sun Valley, CA 91352

Light & Sound Design, Inc.   805-499-6886
1415 Lawrence Drive
Newbury Park, CA 91320

Mole-Richardson Co.   323-851-0111
937 N. Sycamore Ave.
Hollywood, CA 90038

Musco Mobile Lighting, Ltd.   818-988-1791
6926 Valjean Avenue
Van Nuys, CA 91406

Ocean, Rose & Associates   323-860-3500
1040 N. Las Palmas Avenue, Bldg. 27
Hollywood, CA 90038

Paladin Cine Rentals   323-851-8222
7356 Santa Monica Blvd.
Los Angeles, CA 90046

Paskal Lighting   323-466-5233
6820 Romaine Street
Hollywood, CA 90038

TM Motion Picture Equip Rentals, Inc.   818-764-7479
7376 Greenbush Avenue
North Hollywood, CA 91605

Vari-Lite, Inc.   818-507-0700
1620 Flower Street
Glendale, CA 91201

GRIP & LIGHTING EXPENDABLES
Birns & Sawyer, Inc.   323-466-8211
1026 N. Highland Ave.
Hollywood, CA 90038

Castex Rentals   323-462-1468
1044 N. Cole Avenue
Hollywood, CA 90038

Expendable Supply Store   818-525-5350
3111 N. Kenwood Street
Burbank, CA 91505

The Great American Market   323-461-0200
826 N. Cole Avenue
Hollywood, CA 90038

Hollywood Rental Co., Inc.   818-768-8018
7848 N. San Fernando Rd.
Sun Valley, CA 91352

Mole-Richardson Co.   323-851-0111
937 N. Sycamore Ave.
Hollywood, CA 90038

POST-PRODUCTION HOUSES

Absolute Post, Inc.   818-953-4820
Contacts - Eddie Ackerman, Dan Janetzk
2911 W. Olive Ave.
Burbank, CA 91505

Anderson Video   818-777-7999
100 Universal City Plaza
Building 153
Universal City, CA 91608

Ashfield & Company   213-462-3231
Contact - Roxanne King
474 Seward Street
Hollywood, CA 90038

Complete Post, Inc.   323-467-1244
Contact - Dan Filice
6087 Sunset Blvd.
Hollywood, CA 90028

Editel/LA   323-931-1821
Contact - Melissa Hagman, Alana Ireland
729 N. Highland Ave.
Hollywood, CA 90038

Encore Video   323-466-7663
6344 Fountain Ave.
Hollywood, CA 90028

525 Post Production   323-525-1234
Contact - Laura Richards
6424 Santa Monica Blvd.
Hollywood, CA 90038

Foto-Kem/Foto-Tronics, Inc.   818-846-3101
Contact - Steve Van Anda
2800 W. Olive Ave.
Burbank, CA 91505

Four Media Company   818-840-7000
2820 W. Olive AVe.
Burbank, CA 91505

LA Digital Post, Inc.   818-508-9969
Contact - Mark Bianchi
Toluca Lake, CA 91602

Pacific Ocean Post   310-458-3300
Contact - Andrea D'Amico, Alix Eglis
730 Arizona Avenue
Santa Monica, CA 90401

The Post Group   323-462-2300
Contact - Rich Ellis
6335 Homewood Avenue
Hollywood, CA 90028

The Post House   323-464-0116
Contact - Jerry Johnson
1311 N. Highland Avenue
Hollywood, CA 90028

Raleigh Studios Post-Production   323-871-5649
Contact - Walter Canton, Mike Donahue
5300 Melrose Ave.
Hollywood, CA 90038

Sony Pictures Studios Post-Production   310-280-5722
Contact - Steve B. Cohen
10202 W. Washington Blvd.
Culver City, CA 90232

Sunset Post, Inc.   818-956-7912
Contact - Steve Buchsbaum
1813 Victory Blvd.
Glendale, CA 91201

ORDER FORM

Fax orders: (818) 222-2389

On-line orders: Captainnemo2@earthlink.net

Postal orders: *GET A REEL JOB*, Angel's Touch Productions, 22906 Calabash Street, Woodland Hills, CA 91364, USA

Please send me_____ copies of the book *GET A REEL JOB*. I understand that I may return any books for a full refund, for any reason, no questions asked, within 30 days from receipt of the book(s).

Company name: _____

Name:_____

Address: _____

City:_____ State:_____ Zip:_____

Telephone: (_____) _____

Sales Tax:
Please add 8.25% for books shipped to California addresses.

Shipping:
$5.00 for the first book and $3.00 for each additional book.

Payment:
_____Check (enclosed)
_____Credit Card:_____Visa_____Mastercard

Card number: _____

Name on card:_____ Exp. date:_____

Signature: _____

ORDER FORM

Fax orders: (818) 222-2389

On-line orders: Captainnemo2@earthlink.net

Postal orders: *GET A REEL JOB*, Angel's Touch Productions, 22906 Calabash Street, Woodland Hills, CA 91364, USA

Please send me_____ copies of the book *GET A REEL JOB*. I understand that I may return any books for a full refund, for any reason, no questions asked, within 30 days from receipt of the book(s).

Company name: _____

Name: _____

Address: _____

City: _____ State: _____ Zip: _____

Telephone: (_____)_____

Sales Tax:
Please add 8.25% for books shipped to California addresses.

Shipping:
$5.00 for the first book and $3.00 for each additional book.

Payment:
_____Check (enclosed)
_____Credit Card:_____Visa_____Mastercard

Card number: _____

Name on card:_____ Exp. date: _____

Signature: _____